TOMATOES

A COUNTRY GARDEN COOKBOOK

TOMATOES

A COUNTRY GARDEN COOKBOOK

By Jesse Ziff Cool

Photography by Deborah Jones

CollinsPublishersSanFrancisco
A Division of HarperCollinsPublishers

First published in USA 1994 by Collins Publishers San Francisco
Copyright © 1994 Collins Publishers San Francisco
Recipes and text copyright © 1994 Jesse Ziff Cool
Photographs copyright © 1994 Deborah Jones
Food Stylist: Sandra Cook
Floral and Prop Stylist: Sara Slavin
Project Direction, Art Direction and Design: Jennifer Barry
Editor: Meesha Halm
The tomato illustration on page 41 is from The Best of the Old Farmer's
Almanac by Will Forpe. Copyright © 1977 by Jonathan David Publishers.
Reprinted with the permission of Jonathan David Publishers.
Library of Congress Cataloging-in-Publication Data
Cool, Jesse Ziff.
Tomatoes: a country garden cookbook / by Jesse Ziff Cool:
photography by Deborah Jones.
p.   cm.
Includes index.
ISBN 0-00-255343-0
1. Cookery (Tomatoes)   I. Title.
TX803.T6C66 1994
641.6'5642--dc20   CIP 93-35625

Acknowledgments

Loving food and seeing it as more than sustenance, as a medium for expression and caretaking, is taught to us; it is not genetic. I am lucky to have two parents, June and Eddie Ziff, who continue to fill my life with love, celebration and a deep passion for food.

I wish to thank Stuart Dickson, the sweetest, juiciest tomato farmer I know, for his support and guidance.

I love to write, but with restaurants and single-parenting at my shirttails, taking on a book has for years seemed impossible. The biggest encouragement came from Eric Mason, my manager at Flea St. Café who, when I returned from a long walk along the bay and announced that I did not want to write a book, threatened to quit. I wrote the book. Thanks also to the staff at Flea St. who supported me during the project.

A very special thanks to Ros Creasy for her invaluable support, friendship and knowledgeable comments on the glossary of this book.

My gratitude to David Vose, Joseph Steinke, Mark Lipscon, the people at Shepherd's Seed Company and all the other farmers, scientists and produce brokers who talked tomato with me; dear friends and recipe testers, Lisa Fenwick, Gary Smith, Kathleen Samuels, Monica Mitchel, Andrena Appleby, Eric Mason, Carry White and her mom; and Beth Hensperger, for her tea bread recipe. Also deep felt thanks to Bob Cool, who has supported me throughout my career.

The visual beauty of this tomato book deserves to be credited to photographer Deborah Jones and food stylist Sandra Cook. They created these luscious images to seduce you into wanting to grab a fork and dive right in.

Thanks also to my editor Meesha Halm, who guided me through the insecurities of writing, making it a worthwhile and very exciting adventure to produce this book.

Collins and the photography team would also like to thank Jeri Jones and Helga Sigvaldadottir, photo assistants; Kathleen Fazio and Vicki Roberts Russell, food styling assistants; Kristen Wurz, design and production coordinator; and Jonathan Mills, production manager. Special thanks to Stuart Dickson at Stone Creek Farm for all his tomatoes; Mary Novak; Iron Horse Vineyards in Sonoma County; and San Francisco merchants Biordi Italian Imports, Fillamento, RH and Sue Fisher King.

CONTENTS

INTRODUCTION

In my hometown of Greensburg, Pennsylvania, there was heavy competition over the growing of tomatoes. It was a really big deal and my dad took it very seriously. The main rivalry concerned who had the first ripe tomato in town. The second was deciding which tomato looked the most perfect. And the third, for which my dad always took the prize, was whose tomatoes tasted best.

Dad's tomato mentor was Dan Antonucci, an Italian who showed him how tomatoes were grown in the Old Country. Dan gave my dad heirloom seeds brought from Italy by his family in the early 1900s. Some of the seeds were varieties that no one could identify. Dad would save the seeds from his favorites, and year after year he produced the meatiest Romas, plumpest little yellow pears and most luscious big bumpy beefsteaks in western Pennsylvania.

He chose the sunniest spot in the corner of our backyard to grow his beauties. A small brick wall held up a 10-foot by 10-foot raised bed dedicated to his tomatoes. It was on this wall that I sat every summer, saltshaker in hand, awaiting my first bite of warm ripe tomato. That moment became a sacred yearly ritual for my father and me.

While planting his tomato seeds, my dad was actually planting the seeds of my lifelong commitment to sustainable agriculture and organic farming. He took great pride in the fact that he followed Mr. Antonucci's old-fashioned gardening practices. He scoffed when all the other neighbors used pesticides and artificial fertilizers. My dad was convinced that this was why his tomatoes tasted better than any others, except Dan Antonucci's, of course.

As a child, I devoured tomatoes like they were juicy peaches. My mom made me stay outside to eat them because I loved the feel of the juices dripping down my chin. The sweet smell of the tomato intoxicated me as well, and I hoped that rinsing my hands would not make it go away. When I wanted to splurge, I made my favorite sandwich of thick slices of beefsteak tomato, homegrown onions, lettuce and mayonnaise on soft white bread. I was in paradise.

Toward the end of the growing season, we ate lots of unripe green tomatoes. Mom would bread and fry them. Dad dipped them in garlic and oil and grilled them next to rib eye steaks. My brothers hated them; I couldn't get enough.

The exact origin of tomatoes remains a mystery but there is reason to believe that the original tomato came from Peru. Under the name of *tomatl,* it was taken to Mexico by migrating Peruvians. It found its way to Italy via the explorations of Christopher Columbus.

The original tomato was probably yellow fleshed because the Italians referred to it as *pomo d'oro,* meaning "apple of gold." Leave it to them to marry the tomato with pasta, a combination that would eventually influence cuisines around the world.

The French, with their passion for food and romantic notions, took it a step further. They incorrectly translated the word as *pomo d'amore,* meaning "apple of love." It was shipped to England under that same name, becoming an extremely desirable commodity of the powerful and wealthy. Rumor was that the tomato was a powerful aphrodisiac. History books have recorded Sir Walter Raleigh giving Queen Elizabeth a nice, big, juicy tomato as a gesture of his affection. (Who needs roses?)

When the early settlers came to the New World, they brought tomato seeds. Whether it was Puritan ethic (bring the aphrodisiac, but don't dare consume it) or the fact that the settlers landed in chilly New England, the tomato was not grown to be eaten until the late 1800s.

It wasn't until Henry J. Heinz bottled tomato catsup in 1876 that this vegetable gained widespread acceptance in the United States. Today, tomatoes, along with potatoes and lettuce, are the top-grossing vegetables in the United States.

The botanical name for the tomato is *Lycopersicum.* Along with the potato and the eggplant, it is a member of the Night Shade/Solanaceae family.

Originally classified as a fruit, the tomato is now generally accepted in the modern world as a vegetable. The transition from a fruit to a vegetable took place for commercial reasons in 1893. Prior to that, tomatoes, along with all other fruit, were exempt from taxes in the United States. When this came to the attention of the Supreme Court, a judge, possibly with increased government revenues in mind, mandated that the tomato was indeed not a fruit at all because it was eaten at mealtime rather than as a dessert. He thus legally classified it as a vegetable and thus it has remained.

GLOSSARY

Availability: Tomatoes are a summer crop. Sun-ripened tomatoes are grown in California from June through late October. Elsewhere, the temperature and the amount of sunlight will determine when varieties are available from nearby farms and gardens.

Imported tomatoes are available year-round. When out of season, they typically lack taste and texture. Most are picked while still green, then ripened upon delivery after being gassed with ethylene. Their red skins seduce the cook into thinking their flavor might match their vibrant color.

Hydroponic and greenhouse tomatoes are grown in mineral solutions instead of soil. This method of growing typically uses significant dosages of artificial chemicals. They are also available year-round, but lack texture and flavor.

Selecting: Choose tomatoes that have bright, shiny skins. There should be no evidence of mold on either the blossom or the stem end. Discoloring and bruising can affect the texture of the flesh. If you buy greenish tomatoes, they must be ripened in a warm, sunny place, but the flavor will not be as good as vine-ripened ones. In general, avoid broken skins and overly soft tomatoes unless you are making a sauce. The softest, ripest ones can be the best for tomato sauces or juice.

On the other hand, don't be afraid to purchase odd-shaped tomatoes that are bumpy, have growth lines or have large, expansive eyes. They are the old-garden type and may have the finest, most delicious flavors you have ever tasted.

Canned versus Fresh: I recommend using fresh tomatoes only during the two to five months they are in season, grown locally and, most importantly, fully vine-ripened. Out of season I suggest using canned whole, puréed or stewed tomatoes as well as prepared sauces. It is impossible to get a good-tasting sauce or salad ingredient when the tomato is lacking. Canned tomatoes are typically processed at the height of the season, when they are most flavorful. You usually get what you pay for. A few extra pennies for a quality canned product, especially if it is organic, is well worth the added expense.

Storing: Do not store tomatoes in the refrigerator unless they are near spoilage or have broken skins. It affects their flavor. If for some reason you must, be sure to allow them to warm to room temperature before serving them on salads or appetizers.

Place unripe tomatoes, not touching, on a sunny windowsill or in a warm spot. Store ripe ones in a well-ventilated basket or bowl, checking daily for spoilage or moisture leaks. Remove any overripe tomatoes with broken skins.

If you grow your own tomatoes, here is a technique that could give you fresh tomatoes long after the plants are pulled out of the ground. Before the first frost, hang the whole plant, ripe and unripe tomatoes alike, upside down in a cool, dark place. The tomatoes will ripen slowly, extending accessibility for weeks.

Cooking: Tomatoes can differ dramatically in size, water content and flavor. The first, most important thing you must do is taste, touch and get to know the tomato. If it is full of natural sugars and acids, go lightly on your seasoning, giving center stage to the tomato itself. If it lacks flavor, you might want to go a little heavier on spices, herbs and all seasoning. When preparing a cooked sauce, if the tomato isn't imparting the zip you expect, try using either brown sugar, red wine, strong olive oil, lemon juice or balsamic vinegar as flavor enhancers. Do not use aluminum or copper pots when cooking with tomatoes. The acid in the tomato creates a reaction that will discolor the sauce and the pot. As far as water content, use your good judgment, adjusting liquid quantities according to the individual tomato.

Freezing: Freeze tomatoes when you don't have time to can them. The tomatoes should be thoroughly ripe. There are two techniques for freezing. One is to freeze them uncooked, either whole or cut into pieces. The other is to cook the tomatoes into a simple sauce and then freeze it. Fresh frozen tomatoes must be drained of water before adding them to soups or sauces. A frozen cooked tomato releases less water than one frozen fresh. Unripe green tomatoes will freeze, but, like apples, will have a mushy texture when thawed.

Drying: When sun drying tomatoes, begin with the best tomatoes you can find. The flavors and aromas of the fresh tomatoes will be intensified in the sun-dried product. There are two methods to achieve this.

Oven drying: Wash, core and slice the tomatoes 1/4-inch thick and place on a ventilated rack in a 150 degrees F. oven for approximately 6 to 8 hours, depending upon the size of the tomato slices.

Sun drying: Wash, core and slice the tomatoes approximately 1/4-inch thick. Place on screens or well-ventilated racks in a very hot, sunny spot. Cover lightly with cheesecloth to protect from insect infestation. Turn the tomato slices daily. It should take approximately 3 days to sun dry the tomatoes. If you live in an area that has cool nights, be sure to bring them inside to avoid moisture.

With either method, tomatoes are sun-dried when most of the moisture is dehydrated and the texture becomes somewhat leathery. They should taste intense and sweet. The less moisture, the less chance of spoilage. Moister sun-dried tomatoes that have not been treated with preservatives should be kept in airtight containers or in the freezer.

For safety's sake, freeze all sun-dried tomatoes for at least 48 hours. This will kill any visually undetectable insect larvae in the sun-dried tomatoes. Sun-dried tomatoes will last up to 6 months.

Peeling: Core the top end of the tomato and cut an X in the bottom end. Bring a large pot of water to a boil and immerse the tomato in the water for 15 to 30 seconds. The riper the tomato, the less time it should take to loosen the skin. Transfer immediately to an ice bath. Drain and remove skins. To peel frozen whole tomatoes, remove from the freezer and submerge directly in the boiling water for approximately 15 seconds and transfer to an ice bath. The skins should slip off easily.

Seeding: The tomato does not have to be peeled in order to be seeded. But, if you are both peeling and seeding, it is more practical to peel first and seed second. To remove the most amount of seeds, the tomato must be cut diagonally somewhere between the stem and the butt. If you are going to be chopping or puréeing the tomato, slice through the center. If you need to keep its shape, cut as near to the stem as possible. To remove the seeds, invert the tomato over the sink, squeeze gently and tap against the rim or simply scoop out the seeds with a small spoon. If the tomatoes are very ripe, the seeds will come out more easily.

Canning: To prevent any threat of botulism, you must not take any shortcuts when canning tomatoes. Be sure to choose the most flavorful on the market. Peel and seed the tomatoes. Leave them whole, or cut into slices or wedges. If the tomatoes are underripe, boil them until they become juicy, approximately 5 to 10 minutes. Ladle uncooked or cooked tomatoes into sterilized jars allowing approximately a 1/2-inch space at top. Proceed with canning as described in any general cookbook. Store in a cool, dark place.

Char Roasting: Rub the tomato skins with olive oil and place on a hot grill or under a broiler, turning often until skins blacken and begin to split. Or skewer tomatoes on the end of a long-handled fork and rotate over a gas flame until blackened. Place a colander over a glass bowl. Put charred tomatoes in colander and cover with aluminum foil. Allow the tomatoes to cool, then skin and seed them. If you are making a vegetable stock, the addition of charred tomatoes, skins and all, will impart a lightly smoky flavor.

Familiar Tomato Terminology:

Tomato Concassé: Concassé is the simple process of coarsely chopping a vegetable. To make tomato concassé, peel, seed and coarsely chop ripe tomato flesh. Season with salt and use as a simple sauce for pasta or vegetables. Tomato concassé is often used as a base for more complex sauces.

Tomato Coulis: Coulis is a classic French term for chopped tomato pulp that is salted and drained over a colander to extract as much water as possible. The tomato flavor is intensified through this process. Typically it is then puréed into a slightly chunky sauce. Use it as a simple sauce, hot or cold or season with fresh herbs, spices, salt or pepper. Coulis freezes well and, like concassé, is perfect on its own or as a base for more complicated sauces and stews.

Tomato Paste: Basically, tomato paste is whole tomatoes that are simmered slowly (with the optional addition of celery or onions) until very thick. Strain through a food mill or fine sieve, then return to the stove and cook over low heat, stirring constantly to the consistency of a thick, concentrated paste. Add to soups or sauces to impart a depth of flavor.

Tomato Salsa: The Spanish word *salsa* translates as "sauce" in English. Mexican-style salsas can be hot or cold. Typical ingredients in a tomato salsa are ripe tomato pulp, chopped red onions or green onions, cilantro and chilies. Adding lime juice, avocado, cucumber, garlic or ground cumin will transform an ordinary tomato salsa into your own creation.

Additional Growing Terminology:

Conventional: Product grown under conditions adhering to federal Food and Drug Administration guidelines. These guidelines permit the use of chemical amendments and pesticides approved for use in the United States.

Heirloom: Varieties of tomatoes that have been grown for 50 years or more and that are open-pollinated. These pure varieties reproduce the same flavor and consistency year in and year out and have an "old-fashioned" tomato taste that many people think hybrid varieties lack.

Hybrid: Plants that are produced by cross-parenting plants differing in more than one gene. In tomatoes, hybridization is aimed at increasing flavor, productivity and disease resistance. Seeds of hybrid tomatoes must, by law, be labeled as such on seed packets.

Hydroponic: Tomatoes grown in water to which nutrients are added, not grown in soil. Hydroponic tomatoes are typically grown in greenhouses.

Organic: No synthetic chemicals are used to amend the soil or to treat the plant. Strict specifications established by state governments and organizations set the guidelines for what is classified as organic. Call your state or county agricultural department for more information.

Nutritional Information: Tomatoes are low in carbohydrates and contain no fat. One cup of chopped tomatoes is approximately 50 calories, provides up to 60 percent of the adult daily requirement of vitamin C and is loaded with vitamin A. Tomatoes are also high in calcium and potassium. However, cooking them will diminish the vitamin and mineral content.

Health Implications: The tomato is a natural antiseptic. Contrary to popular opinion, ample consumption of them can improve the skin and, like garlic and onions, purify the blood. Tomatoes are also believed to relieve gas in the stomach. The high vitamin C content of tomatoes helps prevent colds, and a nicotine acid in tomatoes presumably helps reduce cholesterol in the blood.

Yields and Measurements: If you shop at farmers' markets or grow your own tomatoes, you know that there is no standard-sized tomato. Many beefsteak tomatoes can weigh up to a pound and a half. This is a list of information gathered from traditional cookbooks to help you follow most recipes when they call for specific measurements.

One pound of tomatoes equal:

2 large, 3 medium or 4 small tomatoes

20 to 24 standard cherry tomatoes

1 cup chopped tomato pulp

28 ounces canned tomatoes equal:

3 pounds fresh tomatoes

3 cups chopped fresh tomatoes

The tomatoes in this glossary are listed by their varietal name. However, tomatoes are often referred to in the market as beefsteaks and slicers. These descriptions pertain to the shape and size of the tomato. A beefsteak is any large, pumpkin-shaped, irregularly-sized tomato. The Ace 55 and Marvel Stripe are examples of a beefsteak tomato. A slicer is any uniformly-shaped tomato that would allow you to cut a maximum of even slices out of it. Early Girl and Dona are examples of a slicer tomato. In addition, different tomato farmers often call the same tomato by a different name. For cooking purposes, however, the ripeness, flavor and texture of the tomato, and not it's name, is what really matters.

Reds:

Ace 55: Large, globe-shaped, low-acid tomato. Thick walls and solid, meaty flesh. One of the most common commercially grown tomatoes. Use on sandwiches, salads and for cooking. It is not recommended for canning because of its low acidity.

Better Boy: One of the most popular hybrids. Looks like the classic, smooth, bright red tomato with plenty of flavor. Meaty and juicy fruits. Great eaten raw, canned or in sauces.

Celebrity: Winner of the 1984 All-American Selection competition. Exceptionally flavorful, medium-sized fruit with outstanding disease-resistant qualities. Globe-shaped, all-purpose tomato.

Dona: Deep red, medium-sized, slightly flattened shape. Meaty, rich, juicy flavor. Exceptionally sweet, yet balanced acidic qualities. Bears a lot of fruit. Good all-round tomato for raw use or in cooking.

Early Girl: One of the first red slicing tomatoes to appear on the market. Round, medium-sized, full flavored, bright red color. Great for the home gardener. Great for salads, sandwiches and for cooking. A good tomato for sun drying. Considered an heirloom variety.

Red Currant: Tiny, 1/4-inch, grape-sized tomatoes that grow in loose clusters and are often marketed when still on the vine. Crunchy, sweet and fruity. Good for salads, pickling and snacks. Available in yellow as well as red, but the yellows are acid-free and milder in flavor. Grows well in all climates, bearing heavily all summer. Fresh eating only.

Roma: Improved paste tomato with fuller flavor. Bright red, thick walls with few seeds. Great for the home gardener because it produces a lot of fruit. Perfect for canning, catsup and sauces.

Sweet 100: Grown in large clusters, these are low-acid, cherry-sized red tomatoes with mouthwatering sweet and juicy flavor. Best for salads or appetizers. Hold up well to quick sautés or skewered on vegetable kabobs.

Yellows:

Lemon Boy: Medium- to large-sized, very juicy, truly yellow tomato. Sweet, delicate and mild flavored with low acid. Best for fresh eating such as in salads and sandwiches, but very good in cold soups such as gazpacho or cold purées.

Yellow Pear: Available in both yellow and red. Small, 1- to 1 1/2-inch, clear yellow, mild-flavored, pear-shaped tomato.

Can be exceptionally sweet. Low-acid, mild flavor. Good for salads and pickling. Considered an heirloom variety.

Yellow Plum: Available in both yellow and red. Small, cherry-type, plum-shaped tomato with a very mild, juicy, sweet flavor. Great for fresh eating, jams or marinated salads.

Golden/Oranges:

Caro Rich: Large beefsteak type with deep golden-orange flesh. Well-known for its high content of beta-carotene. Low in acid with a mild, sweet, delicate flavor. Grows best in Mediterranean-style climates. Good for fresh eating, cold soups and sauces.

Golden Jubilee: Large, bright orange flesh and skin. Juicy, mild flavor with meaty, thick walls. One of the best orange tomatoes. Great for fresh eating, sauces, salsas and juices. Considered an heirloom variety.

Goldy: One of the oldest varieties still being grown. Giant, pumpkin-shaped with golden skin and fine mild flavor. Nonacidic with thick, meaty walls. Great for fresh eating in salads, sandwiches, sauces and salsas. A very good grilling tomato. Considered an heirloom variety.

Greens:

Green Grape: Cherry- to small plum-sized, green with golden-green skin when ripe. Very sweet and considered by many the tastiest of the small tomatoes. Great for salads and appetizers. Use in marinades or skewered on kabobs.

Green Zebra: Green- and yellow-striped skin when ripe, with a light green, very soft interior. Very sweet, lemony, flavorful. Good slicing tomato. Best used fresh on salads or sandwiches.

Unripe Green Tomato: Any tomato that has not begun to color. Great for pickles, pies, grilling and frying.

Multicolored/Miscellaneous:

Marvel Stripe/Big Rainbow: One of the most beautiful tomatoes around. Can grow to be 1 or 2 pounds each. Irregularly shaped, red and yellow variegated skins with golden-, fuschia- and rose-colored flesh. Very sweet and juicy. Great for grilling, broiling, in salads or on sandwiches. Fine for sauces, but the beauty of the flesh is often lost in the preparation. Considered an heirloom variety.

Tomatillo: Some say this was the original tomato originating in Central America. Others say it isn't a tomato at all, but, because of its seed pattern, a member of the gooseberry family. Although tomatillos can ripen to yellow, they are generally used while still green. Semitart flavor. Used in sauces and as a thickener in many Mexican recipes. Tartness produces a unique, refreshing salsa. Purple tomatillos, which are smaller than the green with a purple skin and interior, are now available.

White Beauty: Large, meaty, low acid, with a high sugar content. Beautiful white skin and creamy white flesh. Because of its sweetness, great eaten raw or cooked in sauces, soups and purées. Considered an heirloom variety.

Ace 55

Celebrity

Better Boy

Dona

Early Girl

Roma

Sweet 100

Red Currant

Green Grape

Green Zebra

Unripe Green Tomato

Lemon Boy

Yellow Pear

Yellow Plum

Caro Rich

Golden Jubilee

Goldy

Marvel Stripe

Tomatillo

White Beauty

Growing Your Own Tomatoes: Nothing compares to the first bite of a warm, just-picked, homegrown, vine-ripened tomato. Many believe this experience is as near to Nirvana as one gets. And luckily, it's relatively easy to grow a great tomato.

First, choose your tomato varieties carefully. Be sure they have a growing season that fits your geographical location. Tomatoes that bear fruit early have a short growing season and are better suited for people who live where the summers are shorter. Buy tomato varieties with usage in mind. Do you want to cook them or do you serve them raw most of the time? Are you planning to can the tomatoes? Choose accordingly.

Tomatoes need good soil. Run your fingers through it. Be sure it is not heavy and is high in organic matter. There must be good drainage so the plants do not rot.

Try using as much organic fertilizer and soil amendments as possible when growing your tomatoes. Not only for health and environmental reasons, but I believe they yield the best flavor. Ask for the organic option on your next trip to your garden supply store. In addition, it is a good idea to fertilize mid-season with fish emulsion. If you have trouble finding organic tomato food, call your local University Extension Agency listed in your phone book under county offices.

Start your tomato seeds indoors in a warm spot. Keep well watered. Once the seeds germinate (approximately 1 to 2 weeks), it is imperative that they be transferred to a very bright, sunny spot or allowed to grow under grow lights.

Long, fairly hot days are a key to growing a successful tomato crop. Choose a spot in your garden or yard where the plant will get as much full sunlight as possible. They need a minimum of 8 hours of full sunlight a day.

When the soil outdoors has warmed up and there is no danger of frost, transfer the baby plants to prepared beds or planting containers.

Tomatoes need a balance of sunshine and water. A real trick to growing a great tomato is how it is watered. Keep the soil moist but do not overwater, which can cause plants and roots to mildew and rot.

Gardeners in arid climates can experiment with the time-honored Mediterranean style of gardening and cut back watering once the fruits have begun to color. It will cause stress to the plant, which may result in some rotting and possible burning from the sun, but the trade-off is a greatly improved flavor.

To ensure that your healthy tomato plants stay that way, pull out any diseased plants. Do not put these plants in your compost pile, as whatever is ailing the plant may reappear in the soil created through your composting.

If you don't have a spot in your garden, you can still grow tomatoes in containers. Choose a spot with full sunlight and an oversized container so that the roots can reach deep into the soil. Follow the same growing practices suggested in the preceding paragraphs, except you'll need to fertilize more often.

OPENERS

When friends stop by, there is nothing nicer than to welcome them with a cool drink or a bit of inviting food. This gesture of goodwill can set the stage for all that follows.

Sandwiches can make great appetizers. Cut them into quarters or slices and arrange them on a flat basket or platter for finger food at its best. The tomato, in all its juicy splendor, is at home when positioned on a piece of fresh, earthy bread.

On the other hand, bread is not necessary to bring out the best in a tomato. Herb-Crusted Tomato, Ham and Gruyère Stacks are basically tomato sandwiches, hold the bread.

In many of these opener recipes, chopped or puréed tomatoes are called for. The recipes for salsa, concassé and coulis will be sensational if the tomato is outstanding. If the tomato is inferior, your final dish will reflect this. Substituting top-quality Italian or domestic, organic, canned tomatoes might be the best option.

Recently, heirloom varieties of tomatoes are reappearing on the market in shades of red, gold, pink, green and even white. Try using ripe green tomatoes in the Oysters with Spiced Concassé. Experiment with golden tomatoes in the Cream of Roasted Tomato Soup. When following the recipes in this chapter and the ones to follow, use your own whimsy in deciding the tomato color.

Cream of Roasted Tomato Soup with Parsley Croutons

Roasting tomatoes imparts a sweet quality unlike any other cooking technique.
Use ripe, firm tomatoes so that they don't get soft too quickly.

2 pounds large ripe tomatoes
Olive oil to coat tomatoes
8 shallots
1 small carrot
1 small fennel bulb
3 tablespoons unsalted butter
2 cups chicken or vegetable stock
5 to 6 sprigs fresh tarragon
5 to 6 sprigs fresh parsley

Salt and freshly ground black pepper, to taste
1 cup heavy cream

Parsley Croutons:
12 thin slices baguette
Olive oil to generously coat both sides
*   of each piece of baguette*
3 cloves garlic, cut in half
1/2 cup Teleme cheese, grated
1/4 cup chopped fresh parsley

Preheat the oven to 425 degrees F. Cut tomatoes in half, seed them and coat with olive oil. Place tomatoes in a shallow baking dish and bake for 30 minutes, turning every 10 minutes, until the skins begin to darken and blister. Remove from oven and let cool. Remove the skins and reserve pulp and all the juices.

Coarsely chop the shallots, carrot and fennel. Melt butter in a medium saucepan over medium heat and sauté chopped vegetables until they are very soft. Add the stock and herbs and simmer over low heat for 30 minutes. Add the tomato pulp and reserved tomato juices. Remove the herb sprigs. At this time, you can either purée the soup or, if you like a smoother soup, run the pulp through a food mill or fine sieve. Season with salt and pepper and extra herbs if you like. Keep warm over low heat.

Lower the oven to 400 degrees F. To make the parsley croutons, brush both sides of baguette slices with olive oil and place on a baking sheet. Rub one side of baguette with garlic. Sprinkle with cheese and parsley and bake until brown.

Add the cream to the soup and heat until warm. Ladle soup into warm bowls and float 3 parsley croutons on top of each bowl. Serve with oversized soup spoons and a glass of Chianti classico. *Serves 4*

Red and Gold Gazpacho with Cucumber Salsa and Crème Fraîche

This version of the classic Spanish dish is thick, herbaceous and, with the use of two different colored tomatoes, exceptionally beautiful. I like my gazpacho chunky. If you like yours smoother, use a blender or food processor to purée ingredients. I like to keep the two colors of tomatoes separate, but, if you're really in a hurry, combine the red and gold tomatoes for an equally fabulous-looking, confetti-like soup.

1 1/2 pounds large golden tomatoes
1 1/2 pounds large red tomatoes
1 medium red onion
1 medium red bell pepper
2 celery stalks
1/4 cup extra virgin olive oil
2 cloves garlic, finely chopped
2 to 3 tablespoons chopped basil or chervil (optional)
1/4 to 1/2 cup chopped fresh cilantro
2 green onions, finely chopped
1/3 to 1/2 cup rice wine vinegar
1 to 2 teaspoons Tabasco sauce, or to taste
Salt, to taste
Freshly ground black pepper, to taste

Chopped fresh jalapeño or dried red chili flakes,
    to taste
Tomato juice or chicken stock, to thin soup (optional)

Cucumber Salsa:
1 medium cucumber, seeds removed
1/4 cup tightly packed cilantro, finely chopped
1/8 cup coarsely chopped red onion
1 teaspoon ground cumin
1 teaspoon finely chopped red or green
    jalapeño pepper
Juice of 1 lime
Salt, to taste

Crème fraîche, for garnish

Be sure the tomatoes are very ripe and juicy. Seed and peel them, reserving any juices to use later to thin out the soup. Separate the golden and the red tomatoes. Coarsely chop the onion, bell pepper and celery. In a medium bowl, combine onion, bell pepper and celery with olive oil, garlic, basil, cilantro, green onion, vinegar, Tabasco, salt, pepper and chilies. Divide this mixture in half, placing it in 2 bowls. In one bowl, add the red tomatoes and in the other, the golden tomatoes.

Use tomato juice or chicken stock to thin each colored soup to desired thickness. Chill for 30 minutes.

While the soup is chilling, prepare the cucumber salsa by coarsely chopping cucumber and cilantro. Add the remaining ingredients. Makes approximately 1 1/2 cups, enough for leftovers to use at another meal as a garnish over grilled fish.

To serve, using 2 ladles, simultaneously pour a ladle of each colored gazpacho into a bowl. They should come together at the center of the bowl, without mixing together. Top with a generous spoonful of cucumber salsa and a dollop of crème fraîche or sour cream.
Serves 4 to 6 generously

Bloody Mary

*Once you've tasted this fresh version of a Bloody Mary, it's tough to settle for anything less.
It's relatively easy to make your own tomato juice, but, if time prohibits, the remaining fresh ingredients
will nonetheless produce a superior cocktail, even using canned juice.*

32 ounces fresh tomato juice (from approximately
    6 pounds of tomatoes)
4 tablespoons finely chopped red onion
1 red or green jalapeño, finely chopped
4 tablespoons finely chopped cucumber (optional)
Juice of 2 limes
1 to 2 tablespoons Worcestershire sauce

Salt, to taste
Freshly ground black pepper, to taste
6 jiggers vodka
Tabasco sauce, to taste
4 celery stalks, for garnish
1 lime cut into quarters, for garnish
4 cooked jumbo prawns, chilled, for garnish

To prepare the tomato juice, begin with very ripe, juicy tomatoes. The better the flavor of the tomatoes, the better the juice. For every quart of juice, you will need approximately 2 quarts of fresh tomatoes.

Chop the tomatoes coarsely. Place the tomatoes in a stainless steel pot and bring to a simmer over low heat. Cook until the tomatoes soften completely and their juices are released. Remove from heat, cool, and run the tomatoes and juice through a food mill, fine sieve or juicer to remove the seeds and skin. Pour the tomato purée into a bowl and let stand for approximately half an hour. Tomatoes that contain significant amounts of water may separate causing the water to rise to the top. If this happens, skim off the water. If necessary, keep skimming as long as the juice keeps separating. The more water you remove, the thicker the tomato juice.

Taste the juice. Remember, this is not canned. It might taste slightly bland without the salt, sugar and citric acid used by commercial canners to bring out the flavors. It should have a heavy, rich tomato aroma, and if the flavor doesn't quite meet your specifications, add salt, sugar or lemon juice to suit your palate.

Refrigerate the juice immediately. It will keep for a few days, but the flavor diminishes with time.

In a 2-quart pitcher, combine the tomato juice with everything but the celery and lime wedges. Pour into 4 tall glasses full of ice and garnish with a celery stalk and lime wedge on each. If you are in a flamboyant mood, top each Bloody Mary with a cooked, chilled jumbo prawn. *Makes 4 tall cocktails*

Oysters with Spiced Tomato Concassé

*The flavor of the ocean in a freshly shucked oyster is
passionately matched with the fine texture and
spicy flavors of tomato concassé. The concassé also
makes a great sauce over blackened rare tuna.*

2 medium ripe tomatoes, peeled and seeded
10 sprigs fresh chervil, leaves only
5 sprigs fresh garlic chives or green onions
2 tablespoons chopped red onion
1 tablespoon horseradish, (if fresh, grated)
4 to 6 tablespoons seasoned rice wine vinegar
1/2 teaspoon Tabasco sauce
Salt, to taste
18 fresh oysters
Chive blossoms, for garnish (optional)

Very finely chop the tomatoes. Finely chop chervil,
chives and red onion. In a small bowl, combine all the
ingredients but the oysters and chive blossoms. Chill.

Just before serving, shuck oysters. Discard any
oysters that are already open. To shuck an oyster,
wash thoroughly, then with the thickest part of the
shell on the bottom, insert a shucking knife into
the hinge end, cutting the hinge muscle. Run the
knife along the perimeter of the shell and separate
both sides. Gently loosen the oyster from the shell
for ease in eating.

Top each oyster with 1 teaspoon of the concassé,
including juices. Arrange on an iced platter and
sprinkle with chive blossoms.

The concassé will keep in the refrigerator for a
day or two. It is a wonderful topping for scrambled
eggs. *Serves 3 to 6*

*Pitcher of Bloody Marys (recipe p. 25) and
Oysters with Spiced Tomato Concassé*

Salsa and Guacamole

Almost everybody likes salsa and guacamole with chips, but salsa never tastes as good as it does in tomato season.

Tomato Salsa:
1 1/2 pounds ripe tomatoes
1 small red onion, finely chopped
1/4 cup finely chopped red bell pepper
2 to 3 tablespoons finely chopped cilantro
2 cloves garlic, finely chopped
1/2 teaspoon (or more) seeded and
    finely chopped jalapeño
Juice of 1/2 lime
Salt, to taste

Guacamole:
2 avocados, coarsely chopped
2 tablespoons grated red onion
Juice of 1 lime
3 tablespoons sour cream
1 teaspoon cumin powder
2 teaspoons finely chopped cilantro
Salt, to taste

To prepare the tomato salsa, seed and coarsely chop the tomatoes. In a medium bowl, blend with the red onion, red pepper, cilantro, garlic, jalapeño, lime juice and salt. Chill.

To make the guacamole, gently mash together the avocados, red onion, lime juice, sour cream, cumin, cilantro and salt in a medium bowl. Allow some chunks of avocado to remain whole. Chill.

Spoon the guacamole into a shallow serving bowl. Cover with approximately 1 inch of the salsa. Garnish with lime wedges and a cluster of cilantro and serve with a basket of chips.
Serves 4 to 8

Jose's Roasted Tomatillo Salsa

Tomatillo salsa is perfect to make during the cooler months, when you can't find juicy ripe tomatoes. This recipe was inspired by Jose Valverde, who has cooked at Flea St. for over 8 years. His technique of roasting the vegetables gives this salsa a smooth taste and a soft velvety texture. It's also great on fish.

1 pound purple or green tomatillos
1 medium yellow onion
1/4 to 1/2 large red bell pepper
1 serrano pepper, with seeds
6 cloves garlic
3 tablespoons extra virgin olive oil
2 green onions
1/4 cup fresh cilantro leaves
Salt and freshly ground black pepper, to taste

Preheat the oven to 375 degrees F.

Remove husks from tomatillos. Coarsely chop the yellow onion and both peppers. In a medium-sized roasting pan, toss the tomatillos, onion, peppers and garlic cloves with the oil. Roast for approximately half an hour, stirring after 15 minutes, until all the vegetables are well softened.

Meanwhile, in a food processor with a metal blade, finely chop the green onions and cilantro.

Remove the roasted vegetables from the oven and while they are still hot, slowly add to the green onions and cilantro in the food processor. Purée until smooth.

Season with salt and pepper. Serve hot or cold. *Makes approximately 2 to 2 1/2 cups*

Zucchini Pancakes with Golden Tomato Concassé

There are times in late summer when it seems like everybody's neighbor is giving
away oversized zucchini and handfuls of very ripe tomatoes. This recipe utilizes them both.
The zucchini pancakes are light, but watch out, it's easy to eat too many.

1 pound golden tomatoes, skinned, seeded and
*   coarsely chopped*
1 1/2 pounds zucchini or any type of summer
*   squash*
1 medium red onion
1 1/2 teaspoons salt
2 cloves garlic, crushed
2 tablespoons chopped fresh mint or basil

1/8 teaspoon ground nutmeg
2 tablespoons grated Parmesan cheese
2 eggs, beaten
3 tablespoons unbleached white flour
Pinch of freshly ground black pepper
Light olive or canola oil, for frying
Salt and freshly ground black pepper, to taste

Place tomatoes in a colander over the sink and strain the juices, saving the juices for future use. Set aside.

Grate the zucchini and onion in a bowl and sprinkle with salt. Let stand for 10 minutes, then squeeze out any excess water. Combine with all the remaining ingredients except for the oil and the tomatoes.

In a heavy-bottomed skillet, heat 1/4 inch of oil until it is smoking and very hot. Drop a 1/4 cup of the zucchini batter into the hot oil. Flatten if necessary. Let the pancake completely brown on one side before flipping to brown the other side.

Remove tomatoes from colander. Salt and pepper them, to taste. Serve tomato concassé on top of or under zucchini pancakes. *Makes 8 to 10 pancakes, serving 4 to 5 as an appetizer*

Herb-Crusted Tomato, Ham and Gruyère Stacks

*This recipe builds on the traditional glory of a grilled ham and
cheese sandwich, taking it a step further by surrounding the appealing, all-American
combination with the sweetness of luscious beefsteak tomatoes.*

8 thick slices of large beefsteak tomato,
   (approximately 1/2-inch thick)
1/4 pound ham or pancetta, thinly sliced
1/4 pound Swiss or cheddar cheese, thinly sliced
2 to 3 teaspoons Dijon mustard
4 large fresh basil leaves

2 eggs
2 tablespoons water
2 tablespoons extra virgin olive oil
2 cups herbed bread crumbs
Salt, to taste
Freshly ground black pepper, to taste

Place the tomato slices on a large plate. Evenly distribute the ham and cheese over 4 tomato slices. On each of the other 4 tomato slices, spread approximately 1/2 teaspoon of mustard and 1 basil leaf. Put a tomato slice with ham and cheese together with one of the mustard and basil tomato slices as you would a sandwich. Repeat with the remaining slices.

Preheat the oven to 400 degrees F.

In a small bowl, beat the eggs lightly with the water and olive oil. In another bowl, place the bread crumbs. Sprinkle the outside of each tomato stack with salt and pepper. Coat the outside of the sandwiches in the whisked egg and olive oil mixture. Completely coat with bread crumbs.

Place the tomato stacks on a lightly oiled baking sheet and bake for approximately 15 minutes or until the bread crumbs are brown and the cheese is melted.

Remove from oven and let stand for 10 minutes before serving. *Makes 4 stacks. Serves 4*

Tomatoes, Onions, Anchovies and Hard-Boiled Egg Sandwiches

*Tomatoes are served on sandwiches year-round.
But when they are not in season, why bother? A mealy,
tasteless tomato can actually detract from the
flavors of all the other ingredients. On the other hand,
when they are in season, nothing compares to the
juicy sweetness a tomato can add to most any sandwich.*

4 slices dark rye bread
3 tablespoons unsalted butter, softened
2 to 3 tablespoons grainy mustard
4 thin slices ripe tomato,
    salted and peppered lightly
4 thin slices Bermuda onion
6 anchovy fillets
2 hard-boiled eggs, thinly sliced

Lay out all 4 slices of rye bread. Butter 2 slices and
generously spread grainy mustard on the other
two. On the buttered slices of bread, arrange the
tomatoes, onions, anchovies and eggs. Top with
the mustard-covered slices. Cut each into 3 mini-
sandwiches and serve with a bottle of dark ale.
Serves 2

*Left to right: Grilled Polenta with Sun-Dried Tomato Pesto
(recipe p. 39), Tomatoes, Onions, Anchovies and Hard-Boiled Egg
Sandwiches, Grilled Eggplant, Tomatoes, Provolone and Pesto
Sandwiches (recipe p. 37), and Marinated Tomatoes and Peppers,
Roasted Garlic Mayonnaise and Brie Sandwiches (recipe p. 36)*

Marinated Tomatoes and Peppers,
Roasted Garlic Mayonnaise and Brie Sandwiches

1 medium tomato, seeded and coarsely chopped
1/2 red or yellow bell pepper,
    seeded and very thinly sliced
3 tablespoons extra virgin olive oil
1 tablespoon balsamic vinegar
Salt and freshly ground black pepper, to taste
8 cloves garlic

Extra virgin olive oil
4 tablespoons mayonnaise
2 slices baguette, 8 inches long,
    cut in half lengthwise
4 to 6 fresh basil leaves
3 ounces of Brie cheese

In a small bowl, combine the tomatoes, peppers, olive oil and vinegar. Add a pinch of salt and pepper. Set aside to marinate.

    To roast the garlic, remove the skin from the cloves and coat with olive oil. Wrap in foil and bake in a 350 degrees F. oven for approximately 15 minutes or until cloves are soft. Mash the garlic and blend with mayonnaise.

Open up the pieces of baguette and spread the mayonnaise generously on one side. Place 2 or 3 leaves of basil on top of each mayonnaise half. Spread the Brie on the other side of the baguettes. Top with the marinated tomatoes and peppers. Close up the sandwiches, cut in half and serve with plenty of napkins. *Serves 2*

Grilled Eggplant, Tomatoes, Provolone and Pesto Sandwiches

4 large slices eggplant
Salt, to taste
Extra virgin olive oil
2 slices baguette, 8 inches long,
* cut in half lengthwise*

1/4 cup pesto
4 slices tomato, cut 1/2 inch thick
4 slices Provolone cheese
* (approximately 3 ounces total)*
2 small handfuls fresh arugula

To grill or roast eggplant, slice into 1/2-inch pieces, salt lightly and let stand for 10 minutes. Brush with olive oil and grill or broil until brown and softened.

Spread pesto evenly on both sides of the baguette. Cover one side with tomato slices and Provolone. Cover the other side with eggplant and top with arugula. Close up the sandwiches, slice in half and serve with a glass of Chianti.
Serves 2

Grilled Polenta with Sun-Dried Tomato Pesto

Ubiquitous on restaurant menus across the country, polenta is easy to make and stores well.
It can be prepared without the butter and cheese if cholesterol and fat are of concern.

Grilled Polenta:
6 cups water
1 teaspoon salt
2 cups polenta
1 stick unsalted butter
1 tablespoon chopped fresh rosemary,
*   basil or oregano*
1/2 cup grated Italian grana cheese
*   (such as Parmesan, Asiago or pecorino)*

Sun-Dried Tomato Pesto:
1 cup sun-dried tomatoes, not packed in oil
Warm water or heated red wine,
*   enough to cover tomatoes*
1/4 cup toasted pine nuts or slivered almonds
2 to 3 cloves garlic
1/4 cup grated Italian grana cheese
4 to 5 fresh basil leaves
3/4 to 1 cup extra virgin olive oil
1 teaspoon salt
Juice of 1/2 lemon
Pinch of dried chilies (optional)

In a heavy-bottomed, 3-quart saucepan, bring the water to a boil. Add salt and gradually stir in the polenta. Over low heat, stir frequently until the polenta thickens, approximately 15 to 30 minutes. It should become thick and creamy. The more you cook the polenta, the smoother it becomes. Stir in the butter, herbs and cheese. Pour warm polenta into a lightly oiled baking sheet or shallow roasting pan. Cover and refrigerate until thoroughly chilled.

While the polenta is cooking, prepare the sun-dried tomato pesto. Soak the sun-dried tomatoes in warm water or red wine until plump, approximately 10 minutes. Drain off liquid. In a blender or food processor fitted with a steel blade, purée the sun-dried tomatoes with the nuts and garlic. Add the cheese and basil and process. Gradually add the olive oil, attempting to create a smooth sauce the texture of thick mayonnaise. Season with salt, lemon juice and chilies, if desired. *Makes approximately 2 cups*

Remove chilled polenta and cut into wedges approximately 1/2 inch thick. Brush with olive oil and either grill over mesquite or bake on an oiled baking sheet in a 400 degrees F. oven until brown. To serve, spoon pesto on top of or alongside the polenta wedges. *Serves 6 to 8*

Note: Leftover sun-dried tomato pesto keeps well in the refrigerator for weeks. It is wonderful tossed with pasta and goat cheese. It is delicious served as a tangy sauce over roasted potatoes or as a pizza sauce in combination with fried onions and ricotta cheese.

ACCOMPANIMENTS

Tomatoes lend themselves naturally to the creation of side dishes, salads and accompaniments. Their sweet acidic flavors act as a flavor enhancer. When the markets and gardens are full of tomatoes they are also brimming with a myriad of other summer vegetables. Combining foods that are harvested at the same time has proven to be not only the healthiest approach, but also the tastiest. Tri-Colored Tomato Salad with Beet Croutons is a perfect example of taking a simple, uncooked tomato and showcasing it with seasonal produce.

On the other hand, as cooks we relish the prospect of transforming that simple tomato into a glorious culinary accomplishment. Side dishes are the perfect stage. In this chapter, there are recipes that invite you to spend a little time in your kitchen. Satisfy your soul by putting up a few jars of Tomato Lavender Jam or Fresh Tomato Catsup. With Oven-Roasted Ratatouille or Fried Green Tomatoes with Spicy Aioli and Crisp Bacon, slower cooking and lower heat are necessary to bring out the deep flavors.

Let your imagination and the harvest of the season be your guide, and let tomatoes be the medium from which it all evolves.

Tomato Tarragon Vinaigrette

Adding a whole tomato to any basic vinaigrette will thicken and sweeten it. This recipe is delicious on greens or tossed with white beans such as cannellini beans or Great White Northerns.

1 medium very ripe tomato
2 to 3 cloves garlic
1/2 small red onion, coarsely chopped
3 tablespoons fresh tarragon leaves

1 cup extra virgin olive oil
1/2 cup rice wine vinegar
Salt and freshly ground black pepper, to taste
3 tablespoons sour cream (optional)

Seed and, if you choose, peel the tomato. In a blender or food processor, purée the tomato, garlic, onion and tarragon. Gradually drizzle the olive oil into the purée. Add the vinegar, salt, pepper and sour cream, if desired. Blend thoroughly. *Makes approximately 3 cups*

Fresh Tomato Catsup

Although this homemade catsup might not taste like the commercially produced condiment you are familiar with, its fresh and lively flavors will win you over.

6 pounds ripe tomatoes
1 large red onion
1/4 cup canola oil
1/2 cup loosely packed fresh parsley
2 stalks celery
1 carrot
1 teaspoon mustard seeds

1 cinnamon stick
1 teaspoon whole allspice
1 nutmeg berry
1 1/2 cups malt vinegar
3/4 cup light brown sugar
1 tablespoon molasses

Cut tomatoes and onion into large wedges. In a large heavy-bottomed, nonreactive pot, heat the oil. Add tomatoes, onions, parsley, celery and carrot and stew over low heat for approximately 45 minutes. Stir every 10 to 15 minutes.

Cool and run through a food mill or fine sieve, separating as much thick purée as possible. Discard solids and return purée to pot.

In a few layers of cheesecloth, tie the mustard, cinnamon, allspice and nutmeg. With a hammer or heavy object, break nutmeg and crush spices slightly. Place the spice bag along with the vinegar, brown sugar and molasses in the tomato purée. Simmer over low heat for 2 to 4 hours, depending upon how juicy your tomatoes are. Stir frequently until the mixture thickens. Sterilize pint-sized jars by boiling in hot water or running them through the dishwasher without detergent. Pour catsup into the sterilized pint-sized jars and store in the refrigerator for months. *Makes approximately 4 cups*

Tomato Lavender Jam

This recipe is adapted from Larousse Gastronomique, *the classic French cookbook. The addition of fresh lavender adds a delicate flavor that pairs nicely with cream cheese and crackers or English muffins.*

3 pounds ripe tomatoes
3 pounds granulated sugar

Juice of 2 to 3 lemons
6 sprigs lavender, with blossoms, if possible

Seed and peel tomatoes. In a heavy-bottomed, nonreactive pot, combine all the ingredients and bring to a boil. Lower the heat and simmer slowly until the tomatoes break down and the mixture becomes jelly-like. This will take over an hour. Remove the lavender. Sterilize pint-sized jars by boiling in hot water or running them through the dishwasher without detergent. Place the tomato mixture in sterilized jars, with a sprig of lavender in each. The jam will keep for weeks in the refrigerator. *Makes approximately 6 pints*

Curried Pickled Tomatoes

Pickled tomatoes are very easy to make. You can either use small whole unripe tomatoes or large wedges of big green tomatoes. Pickle them in the fall and give them as an impressive Christmas gift in December.

2 pounds unripe green tomatoes
2 medium yellow onions
4 to 5 whole red chili peppers, fresh or dried
3 to 4 cups seasoned rice wine vinegar
3 bay leaves

3 cloves garlic
1 teaspoon whole allspice
2 tablespoons curry powder
1 tablespoon whole cumin

Sterilize 4 or 5 pint-sized jars by boiling in hot water or running them through the dishwasher without detergent.

If the tomatoes are large, cut into wedges. If they are small, leave whole. Cut the onions into wedges approximately the same size as the tomatoes. Layer the onions and the tomatoes alternatively in the sterilized jars. Place 1 chili in each jar.

Meanwhile, in large, nonreactive pot, bring all the remaining ingredients to a boil for 5 minutes. Strain and pour evenly over the tomatoes. Let cool. Add enough liquid to completely cover vegetables and reach within a 1/2 inch of the top of the jar. Add more vinegar if more liquid is needed. Cover with the lids and store in the refrigerator. Give them a minimum of a few days before eating. Good for at least 2 months in the refrigerator or in a cold cellar. *Makes 4 to 5 pints*

Tomato Garlic Lime Butter

Deceptively simple, compound butters can quickly transform an unadorned entrée into a complex and tasty dish. Melt on top of a fish fillet in lieu of a sauce or use in place of regular butter to enliven a simple sauté.

1 large ripe tomato, peeled and seeded
1 to 2 teaspoons salt
2 sticks unsalted butter, softened
8 to 10 cloves garlic, finely chopped
2 tablespoons lime zest
Juice of 1 lime
1/4 cup finely chopped fresh parsley
2 teaspoons ground cumin
1 fresh jalapeño, seeded and minced

Chop the tomato and sprinkle with salt. Place in a colander and let the juices drain off.* Blend the butter with all the ingredients by hand or quickly process in a food processor. Roll the mixture into a cylinder approximately 1 inch thick in a sheet of parchment paper, waxed paper or plastic wrap. Chill until firm. (Butter can also be frozen for future use.) To serve, slice the log into small rounds. *Makes 1 1/2 cups*

Note: The amount of liquid in tomatoes can vary dramatically. Be sure to squeeze out as much juice as possible before combining it with the butter.

Red Pepper Tomato Butter

Try this melted over polenta, mashed potatoes or an ear of freshly picked steamed sweet corn.

1 large tomato, peeled and seeded
1 teaspoon salt
2 sticks unsalted butter, softened
1/2 cup grated Italian grana cheese
    (such as Asiago or Parmesan)
1/3 cup roasted red peppers,
    chopped and juices squeezed out
4 cloves garlic, finely chopped
1/2 cup finely chopped fresh basil
3 tablespoons whole toasted pine nuts

Chop the tomato and sprinkle with salt. Place in a colander and let the juices drain off.* Blend the butter with all the ingredients by hand or quickly process in a food processor. Roll the mixture into a cylinder approximately 1 inch thick in a sheet of parchment paper, waxed paper or plastic wrap. Chill until firm. (Butter can also be frozen for future use.) To serve, slice the log into small rounds. *Makes 3 cups*

Tomato, Bermuda Onion, Fresh Mozzarella and Three Basil Salad

This is possibly the best way to eat a perfectly ripe, juicy tomato. However, the success of this dish lies entirely in the quality of the ingredients. Don't even bother serving it unless the tomatoes you buy are as sweet as sugar. Use top-quality virgin olive oil and fresh, delicate mozzarella. They're worth a few cents more. If you can find boconcino or small mozzarella balls, they are wonderful. If you can't find three different kinds of basil, the sweet green variety will do just fine.

*3 pounds ripe tomatoes (any color),
 at room-temperature, thickly sliced*
1 medium red onion, very thinly sliced
*1 cup fresh basil leaves (any combination of
 sweet green, purple, lemon, cinnamon,
 Thai or chocolate), coarsely chopped*

*6 to 8 ounces good-quality fresh mozzarella,
 thickly sliced*
1/4 to 1/3 cup extra virgin olive oil
4 to 6 tablespoons balsamic or red wine vinegar
Salt and freshly ground black pepper, to taste
Sprigs of fresh basil

On a large platter, layer the tomatoes, onions and basil as you would a lasagna. Top with the mozzarella. Drizzle with oil and sprinkle with balsamic vinegar. Season with salt and pepper. Garnish with sprigs of basil.
Serves 4

Tri-Colored Tomato Salad with Beet Croutons and Geranium-Scented Soft Cheese

The glory of this dish comes from how creative you can get when cutting the tomatoes to bring out their natural beauty. Slice them, wedge them, halve them or leave them whole. Cluster them together by shape and color to accentuate each tomato's individuality. I adore using the blossoms and leaves of scented geraniums that I grow. They soften the pungency of cheeses. If you don't have access to them, use edible flowers of your choice, and in place of the geranium use a minty herb such as basil, sage or mint. Be sure the blossoms you use are unsprayed and organic.

1 large red onion
2 medium red tomatoes
  (or a basket of red cherry tomatoes)
2 medium golden tomatoes
  (or a basket of yellow cherry tomatoes)
2 medium ripe green tomatoes
  (or a basket of green grape tomatoes)
1/4 to 1/3 cup extra virgin olive oil
4 to 5 tablespoons balsamic or raspberry vinegar

1 to 2 tablespoons chopped fresh sage
2 teaspoons finely chopped garlic
Salt and freshly ground black pepper, to taste
4 to 6 ounces fresh ricotta, soft goat or cream cheese
2 tablespoons chopped unsprayed geranium blossoms
  (or rose, nasturtium or calendula blossoms)
1 to 2 teaspoons chopped scented geranium leaves
  (or substitute fresh basil, sage or mint)
2 medium fresh raw beets (red, golden or chiogga)

Thinly slice the onion and arrange evenly on a large platter. Cut tomatoes however you want, in slices, wedges or, if they are small, in half. Either toss together or cluster by color on top of onions toward the center of the platter. In a small bowl, whisk together the oil, vinegar, sage, garlic, salt and pepper and drizzle over tomatoes. Set aside.

In a small bowl, blend the soft cheese with the blossoms and herbs.

Think of the beets as crunchy, sweet croutons or crackers. Slice them as thinly as possible and spread the ricotta on them. Place them around the outer edge of the platter. Garnish with a beautiful cluster of whole geranium blossoms and leaves. *Serves 4 to 8*

Marinated Cherry Tomatoes over Warm Provolone Garlic Bread

Covering the tomatoes in the marinade is the key to the success of this simple tomato salad.
Spooning the tomatoes over the warm cheese bread creates a rustic dish that is deeply satisfying.

2 baskets cherry tomatoes (yellow pears,
    green grapes, sweet 100s or any available
    miniature ripe tomatoes)
2 green onions, coarsely chopped
1/4 cup finely chopped fresh parsley
1 tablespoon finely chopped fresh rosemary
3 cloves garlic, finely chopped
1/3 cup virgin olive oil
1 tablespoon truffle oil (optional)

3 tablespoons balsamic vinegar
Salt and freshly ground black pepper, to taste

Provolone Garlic Bread:
4 to 6 tablespoons extra virgin olive oil
3 cloves of garlic, finely chopped
4 large, thick slices of crusty white bread
4 slices Provolone cheese, 1/2 ounce each
1/4 cup grated Parmesan or aged Italian grana cheese

In a 2-quart casserole or bowl, mix tomatoes, onions, parsley, rosemary, garlic, oils and vinegar. Cover and marinate at room temperature for at least 1 hour. Season with salt and pepper. Ideally, the mixture should marinate long enough for the tomatoes to crack and burst.

To assemble the Provolone garlic bread, first preheat the broiler. Combine the olive oil and garlic and let stand for 10 minutes. Brush one side of each piece of bread with garlic and olive oil. Broil only brushed side until lightly browned. Cover the toasted side of the bread with 1 slice of Provolone cheese and a generous sprinkling of Italian cheese. Set the bread aside until tomatoes are marinated.

Just before serving, preheat broiler. Toast bread under broiler until cheese is bubbly.

To serve, place a piece of warm, cheesy bread in a shallow soup bowl. Spoon approximately 3/4 cup of the tomatoes and marinade around the edges of the bread. Garnish with more grated Italian cheese. *Serves 4*

Oriental Tomato, Broccoli and Buckwheat Noodle Salad

I use either sun-dried or fresh tomatoes in this salad, depending upon the season. The sun-dried tomatoes add intense sweetness while the fresh tomatoes impart a lightly acidic quality to the dish.

2 to 3 cups broccoli florets, stems chopped,
   lightly steamed, then chilled
1/4 cup rice wine vinegar
1/4 cup soy or tamari sauce
2 tablespoons finely chopped fresh ginger
1 teaspoon finely chopped garlic
1/2 cup roughly chopped green onions

1/2 to 1 teaspoon toasted sesame oil, to taste
1/3 cup coarsely chopped sun-dried tomatoes,
   pre-soaked for 3 minutes in warm water, or
   2/3 cup fresh tomatoes, seeded and chopped
1/4 teaspoon chili flakes (optional)
8 ounces buckwheat noodles
2 teaspoons toasted sesame seeds, for garnish

Place the steamed broccoli in a large serving bowl. In a smaller bowl, blend all the ingredients except the tomatoes, chili flakes, noodles and sesame seeds. Pour the marinade over the broccoli and toss with the tomatoes. Add chili flakes if you want a spicy salad.

In a large pot of salted, boiling water, cook buckwheat noodles as directed on the package. Drain and run under cold water to cool. Divide into 4 portions and put into large soup bowls. Top each with a generous cup of broccoli-tomato mixture, pouring any excess marinade evenly over each bowl. Garnish with toasted sesame seeds. *Serves 4*

Fava Beans with Sun-Dried Tomato Oil and Pancetta on Frisée

If you can't find fresh fava beans, lima beans will work equally well in this salad.

Sun-Dried Tomato Oil:
2 cups extra virgin olive oil
3/4 cup sun-dried tomatoes, coarsely chopped

1 pound shelled fresh fava beans (approximately 5 pounds unshelled)
1/2 cup sun-dried tomato oil
2 teaspoons lemon zest
Juice of 1 lemon

3 cloves garlic, finely chopped
2 tablespoons finely chopped fresh parsley
1 tablespoon finely chopped fresh oregano
1/4 cup coarsely chopped sun-dried tomatoes
Salt and freshly ground black pepper, to taste
1/4 pound pancetta or bacon, thinly sliced
1 head of frisée, washed and outer leaves discarded
Shaved Asiago cheese, for garnish

To prepare the sun-dried tomato oil, heat the olive oil until almost smoking. Pour the hot oil over the tomatoes. Let stand for a minimum of 3 to 4 days. Strain and bottle oil, storing in a cool, dark place. Put the sun-dried tomatoes in a jar and refrigerate for future use. *Makes 2 cups*

Remove the fava beans from the outer pod. If the beans are large, boil them in water for approximately 5 minutes or long enough for the outer shell to pull away from the bean. Pull off shell and taste for tenderness. If necessary, boil for 3 to 5 minutes more or until the beans are soft, but not mushy.

In a large glass or wooden bowl, combine the sun-dried tomato oil, lemon zest and juice, garlic, herbs and sun-dried tomatoes and toss with the warm beans. Marinate for approximately an hour. Season with salt and pepper.

Cut the pancetta into narrow strips and sauté until slightly crisp. Remove from the pan and drain on a paper towel. Break frisée leaves into large bite-sized pieces. Do not tear leaves if they are young and tender. Arrange the frisée on a serving platter and spoon the fava beans and marinade on top. Scatter pancetta and shaved cheese over all. *Serves 4*

Baked Tomatoes Stuffed with Sweet Corn and Crab

Serve these tomatoes as a luscious summery lunch with a simple green salad.
Best served at room temperature, they also travel well as picnic food.

6 medium ripe tomatoes
1 cup fresh corn kernels, blanched for 3 minutes,
    then cooled
1 1/2 cups fresh crab, picked clean
2 tablespoons finely chopped red bell pepper
1/2 teaspoon finely chopped jalapeños or habañeros
2 tablespoons finely chopped green onion or chives
2 teaspoons chopped fresh tarragon

1/2 teaspoon finely chopped lemon zest
1/4 to 1/3 cup mayonnaise
Salt and freshly ground black pepper, to taste
2/3 cup toasted bread crumbs
4 tablespoons unsalted butter, melted
1 tablespoon finely chopped fresh parsley
1/4 teaspoon salt

Preheat oven to 375 degrees F.

With a sharp paring knife, remove tops of the tomatoes, and cut an opening large enough to scoop out the seeds and as much of the juicy inner flesh as possible. Be sure to leave at least 1/4 to 1/2 inch of tomato flesh around the exterior of the tomato to hold in the filling. Turn tomatoes upside down to drain while you prepare the filling.

In a medium bowl, combine the corn, crab, bell pepper, chilies, green onions, tarragon and lemon zest. Moisten with mayonnaise to suit your taste, but enough to hold the mixture together. Season with salt and pepper.

In a small bowl, combine bread crumbs, butter, parsley and salt. Set aside.

Fill the cavities of the tomatoes with crab and corn filling. With your hands, top with a generous amount of the buttered bread crumbs and pat into place.

Place tomatoes upright in a lightly oiled baking dish. Bake for 10 to 15 minutes or until bread crumbs are brown. Allow to cool to room temperature. *Serves 4 to 6*

Fried Green Tomatoes with Spicy Aioli and Crisp Bacon

*When we first started making this dish at my restaurant, we would have to beg farmers
to supply us with unripe tomatoes, especially during the height of the season. At first they thought we were
simply nuts. Then we fried them up a sample and we never had trouble getting them again.*

Spicy Aioli:
1 teaspoon seeded and chopped red or green jalapeño
2 cloves garlic
1 egg yolk
3/4 cup extra virgin olive oil
1/4 teaspoon salt
1/4 teaspoon paprika
Juice of 1/2 to 1 lemon
Cayenne pepper, to taste

3 pounds underripe green tomatoes
3/4 cup unbleached white flour
2 teaspoons salt
1/2 teaspoon freshly ground black pepper
1 1/2 cups yellow or blue cornmeal
1 tablespoon finely chopped fresh rosemary
1 tablespoon finely chopped fresh oregano
2 eggs
Olive oil, bacon fat or a combination of both, for frying
6 strips of bacon, fried to a crisp and crumbled

In a food processor fitted with a metal blade, finely chop the chilies and garlic. Add the egg yolk and purée. Very gradually, stream in the olive oil, processing constantly, until it thickens to a mayonnaise-like consistency. Season with salt, paprika and lemon juice. Taste for spiciness and add a pinch of cayenne should you desire it hotter. Chill until ready to serve. *Makes approximately 3/4 cup of aioli*

While the aioli is chilling, slice the tomatoes into 1/2-inch slices. You can use the stem end as long as you remove the eye.

In a small bowl, combine the flour with 1 teaspoon of the salt and the black pepper. In another small bowl, combine the cornmeal with the remaining salt and the chopped herbs. Whisk the egg with a few tablespoons of water in a third bowl.

Pat the tomatoes dry. Bread each slice as follows: Dust in flour, then the beaten egg and, finally, in the seasoned cornmeal. Set aside.

In a large, heavy-bottomed frying pan or skillet, pour in 1/4 inch oil or fat. Heat over a high flame until it smokes slightly. Turn heat down to medium high. Place tomatoes in hot oil. Brown on one side, approximately 3 to 5 minutes. Turn and brown on the other side. Remove and drain on paper towels. Add more oil if necessary, making sure the oil is very hot each time before putting the tomatoes into it. (If the tomatoes brown before they are soft enough for your taste, place them in a 375 degrees F. oven on a baking sheet and heat for approximately 5 to 10 minutes.)

Serve on a plate with a dollop of spicy aioli and a sprinkling of crispy bacon. You can fry the tomatoes ahead of time and rewarm them in the oven just before serving. *Serves 4 to 6*

Scalloped Potatoes and Tomatoes

This recipe addresses the deep need for simple, nurturing,
old-fashioned "mother food" that exists in many of us, especially me.

1 1/2 to 2 pounds boiling potatoes,
*   preferably new potatoes or yellow Finns*
1 to 1 1/2 pounds ripe tomatoes
1 medium yellow onion
1 stick unsalted butter
2/3 cup unbleached white flour

Salt and freshly ground black pepper, to taste
1 1/2 to 2 cups milk, enough to cover
*   potatoes and cheese*
1 to 1 1/2 cups grated white cheddar cheese
Paprika

Preheat the oven to 375 degrees F.

Do not peel potatoes. Slice the potatoes very thin and place in a bowl. Peel and seed the tomatoes and cut them into approximately 1/8-inch-thick slices. Set aside on a plate. Slice the onion very thin and place in a bowl.

Butter a deep, 3-quart baking dish. In assembling this dish, there should be at least 3 layers of everything. Start by covering the bottom of the dish with a thick layer of the potatoes. Top with a single layer of tomatoes and a handful of onions. Sprinkle liberally with flour, salt and pepper. Dot generously with butter and begin layering again, starting with the potatoes, until you get within 1 inch of the top. Make the last layer tomatoes.

Pour enough milk over the dish to just cover all the ingredients. Top with grated cheese and sprinkle with paprika.

Baking time will depend upon the size and shape of your baking dish. Place a pan beneath the baking dish just in case it bubbles over. Bake for approximately 45 minutes or until the potatoes are soft and most of the milk has been absorbed. Let stand for at least 15 minutes before serving. *Serves 6*

Oven-Roasted Ratatouille

Ratatouille is a classic dish that differs at the hand of every cook. It is the recipe of choice when your neighbor brings you one more basketful of vegetables from her prolific summer garden. Slow oven roasting deepens the flavors. Traditionally, each vegetable is cooked separately. Ros Creasy, author and gardening expert, and I agree that cooking them all together encourages the different vegetables to marry and absorb one another's flavors. Double the recipe if you want leftovers. Toss ratatouille with pasta, serve as a bed under a grilled fish fillet or as an appetizer with plenty of bread, salty olives, aioli and glasses of red wine.

2 to 3 medium tomatoes, seeded
1 medium eggplant (globe, rosa bianca or Japanese)
1 medium red bell pepper, seeded
1 medium yellow onion
2 medium golden summer squash
4 cloves garlic, finely chopped

10 cloves garlic, whole (optional)
1/8 cup extra virgin olive oil
4 to 5 sprigs fresh oregano or sage
1/3 cup fruity red wine
1/4 cup roughly chopped fresh basil
Salt and freshly ground black pepper, to taste

Preheat the oven to 350 degrees F.

Chop tomatoes and all other vegetables into large 1- to 2-inch pieces. Place in a heavy, 3-quart baking dish. Toss the vegetables with all remaining ingredients except basil, salt and pepper. Bake covered for 30 minutes. Remove from oven and baste with pan juices. Cover again and return to oven for another 15 to 30 minutes or until vegetables are very soft. In this dish, the vegetables should not be al dente. Season with basil, salt and pepper. Let cool slightly before serving. *Serves 4 to 6*

MAIN COURSES

One can rarely fail to create a smashing main course with great-tasting tomatoes at one's fingertips. A big, steaming platter of homemade noodles tossed with fruity tomatoes, garlic, basil and olive oil is my idea of paradise.

Many of the dishes included in this chapter call for tomatoes as a main ingredient, such as the Fresh Tomato Lasagna with Wilted Greens, while others, such as the Grilled Lamb Chops with Tomato Pear Chutney and Chili Mashed Potatoes, use tomatoes as one of many flavors to augment the dish in its entirety.

The flavor of a tomato is often described as sweet, fruity or acidic. The palate is naturally pleased by combining these qualities with salty foods. Olives, capers, prosciutto and anchovies bring out the sugar and earthiness of a tomato. The Cappellini with Puttanesca Sauce is a good example of this symbiosis.

I believe tomatoes need to be cooked as little as possible. In your favorite tomato sauce recipe that calls for hours of cooking, take a new approach. Slow cook all the ingredients except the tomatoes, adding them last and just heating them through. This technique will bring out the best of the tomato flavors and minimize vitamin and mineral loss.

Grilled Lamb Chops with Tomato Pear Chutney and Chili Mashed Potatoes

Tomatoes, pears, chilies and potatoes are all in season at the same time.
Bring them together on one plate to create this earthy dinner that is hearty and soul-satisfying.

Tomato Pear Chutney:
2 cups peeled, seeded and coarsely chopped tomatoes
2 cups peeled, cored and coarsely chopped pears
1 medium yellow onion, coarsely chopped
1 cup raisins
2 cups light brown sugar
1 cup cider vinegar
1/4 cup finely chopped fresh ginger
2 tablespoons mustard seed
2 cinnamon sticks
2 spicy chilies, seeded and chopped
2 teaspoons salt

Lamb Marinade:
1 cup virgin olive oil
3 tablespoons red wine
2 tablespoons finely chopped garlic
1 tablespoon finely chopped fresh rosemary
1/2 teaspoon freshly ground black pepper
1 teaspoon salt

4 lamb loin chops, weighing approximately
     5 ounces each

Chili Mashed Potatoes:
2 pounds boiling potatoes, preferably new potatoes
1/2 stick unsalted butter
1/2 cup sour cream
2 tablespoons finely chopped Anaheim or
     serrano chilies
1/4 to 1/2 cup milk, for mashing
Salt, to taste

Finely chopped fresh mint, for garnish

To make the tomato pear chutney, combine all of the ingredients in a 2-quart nonreactive pot. Simmer over low heat for an hour or so or until all fruit is soft and chutney begins to thicken. Remove cinnamon sticks. Place in sterile jars and store in refrigerator or cool, dark place. Chutney will last in the refrigerator up to 6 weeks. *Makes approximately 6 pints*

To marinate the lamb, in a large bowl, combine the olive oil, red wine, garlic, rosemary, pepper and salt. Thoroughly coat the lamb. Allow to marinate for 2 hours or more at room temperature, turning occasionally.

To prepare the chili mashed potatoes, peel the potatoes. Bring a large pot of water to a boil. Boil potatoes until soft. Drain off water. While the potatoes are hot, mash in the butter, sour cream and chilies. Mash thoroughly, adding the milk gradually until light and fluffy. Add salt to taste.

To serve, pan fry or grill the lamb chops. Place approximately 3/4 cup of the mashed potatoes on a dinner plate. Arrange the lamb around the potatoes. Garnish with 2 generous tablespoons of chutney and finely chopped fresh mint. *Serves 4*

Greek Islands Seabass

On a warm summer evening, imagine yourself on a small Greek island watching
sailboats pass by. Although you may not be in the Mediterranean while eating this dish, you can
at least enjoy some of the familiar flavors of this passionate corner of the world.

Herb-Infused Oil:
1/4 to 1/3 cup virgin olive oil
3 sprigs fresh oregano, finely chopped
2 teaspoons lemon zest
3 cloves garlic, finely chopped

1 pound ripe tomatoes, seeded and coarsely chopped
2/3 cup Kalamata or quality brine-cured
*   olives, pitted*
4 to 6 ounces fresh feta cheese or
*   semi-soft Greek cheese*
2 pounds fresh seabass, swordfish or other meaty fish
1/4 cup olive oil, to rub on the fish
Edible blossom petals such as bachelor buttons or
*   chive blossoms, for garnish*
1 lemon, cut into wedges

In a saucepan over medium heat, heat the olive oil for 1 minute. Remove from heat and add the oregano, lemon zest and garlic. Allow the oil to sit at room temperature for at least an hour, or for best results, overnight.

Just before serving, toss the tomatoes with the herb-infused olive oil. Chop the olives coarsely and put in a small bowl. Crumble the feta into another small bowl.

Cut the fish into 4 portions, approximately 8 ounces each. Rub with olive oil and pan fry over very high heat or grill over mesquite. The seabass is done when the flesh turns a translucent, milky color. Do not overcook the fish, especially if it is very fresh.

Place fish on individual plates and top with a few generous tablespoons of tomatoes, olives and feta. Drizzle remaining infused olive oil over each fillet. Sprinkle with edible blossoms and offer lemon wedges on a side plate. Fresh, salted cucumbers and steamed rice go nicely with this dish. *Serves 4*

Top to bottom: Caponata on Bruschetta (recipe p. 68)
and Greek Islands Seabass

Caponata on Bruschetta

*Popular in many Italian restaurants, this dish is a showcase for any
fabulous-tasting tomato. Use different colored tomatoes for an eye-catching presentation.
Caponata is also delicious served as a thick sauce over thin pasta noodles.*

Caponata:
1 medium yellow onion
2 small stalks celery
1 medium eggplant, sliced, salted and drained
    for 15 minutes to remove excess water
1 small red bell pepper, seeded
1/4 cup extra virgin olive oil
1/2 cup red wine vinegar
2 tablespoons light brown sugar
1 tablespoon finely chopped garlic
2 tablespoons pine nuts, toasted
2 or 3 medium tomatoes, seeded, chopped
    and excess juices squeezed out

1/2 cup black brine-cured olives,
    pitted and chopped coarsely
1/4 cup loosely packed fresh basil, finely chopped
3 tablespoons capers
2 to 3 tablespoons raisins, chopped

Bruschetta:
8 slices of baguette or Italian bread,
    (cut approximately 1 inch thick)
Extra virgin olive oil, approximately 1/8 cup
1 tablespoon finely chopped garlic

2 or 3 tablespoons finely chopped fresh parsley

Chop the onion, celery, eggplant and bell pepper into approximately 1/2-inch pieces. In a heavy saute pan over medium heat, cook the vegetables in oil for approximately 10 minutes or until vegetables are soft. Add the vinegar, sugar and garlic and simmer for 5 minutes.

In a small heavy-bottom sauté pan, toss the pine nuts over medium heat until they brown lightly. Let cool.

Transfer the simmering vegetables to a medium bowl and let cool to room temperature. Mix together the tomatoes, cooled vegetables, pine nuts, olives, basil, capers and raisins. Set aside.

To make the bruschetta, preheat oven to 400 degrees F. Place slices of bread on a baking sheet. Combine the olive oil and garlic and let stand for 10 minutes. With a brush, lightly but completely coat both sides of bread. Bake in oven until brown on both sides. You shouldn't have to turn them if your oven is hot enough.

Remove the bruschetta from the oven and generously mound the caponata on top of each. Transfer to a platter, sprinkle with parsley and serve. *Serves 4*

Note: Leftover caponata will keep in the refrigerator for at least a week.

Barbecued Chicken with Charred Tomato Barbecue Sauce

You don't have to use this sauce on chicken. Try it on slices of eggplant or oversized zucchini.
My youngest son loves this barbecue sauce over oven-roasted tofu.

Charred Tomato Barbecue Sauce:
2 pounds very ripe tomatoes
3 thick slices naturally cured bacon
1 medium yellow onion
1/2 cup deveined and coarsely chopped red or green
   bell pepper
1/2 teaspoon chopped habeñero or serrano chili,
   or more to taste
2 cloves garlic, finely chopped
1/2 teaspoon white pepper
1/2 teaspoon freshly ground black pepper

1/2 teaspoon paprika
1 teaspoon ground cumin
1/2 teaspoon ground ginger
1 teaspoon salt
1 tablespoon Worcestershire sauce
1/4 to 1/2 cup red wine vinegar
1/4 to 1/2 cup brown sugar
1 teaspoon orange zest
Salt and freshly ground black pepper, to taste

2 small chickens (approximately 2 to 3 pounds
   each), split in half

Place tomatoes over an open flame or a medium-hot mesquite grill. Cook until the skins blacken and the juices begin to spit from beneath the skin. Transfer the tomatoes to a colander. Strain and let cool. When the tomatoes are cooled, peel, seed and finely chop.

Cut the bacon into small pieces and sauté in a small, heavy-bottomed skillet until crisp. Remove the bacon and set aside. Leaving the fat in the pan, slowly sauté the onion, bell pepper, chili and garlic over low heat until soft. Add the spices and heat for a few minutes over low heat. Add the tomatoes and simmer for at least 30 minutes. Add the Worcestershire sauce, vinegar and brown sugar. If you want a smooth sauce, transfer to a food processor. Add the zest and bacon bits. Season to taste. The sauce can

be kept in the refrigerator for weeks and frozen for several months. *Makes 2 cups of sauce*

Marinate the chicken in the barbecue sauce overnight in the refrigerator.

To barbecue the chicken, light the coals and allow them to burn until they are white, but still give off a medium heat.

Before putting the chicken on the grill, scrape off as much barbecue sauce as possible. (The sugar in the sauce is what will burn on the grill.) Cook the chickens, turning often, for approximately 30 minutes. Insert a knife at the joint of the leg and thigh to check for doneness. (The juices should run clear.)

When the chicken is cooked, remove it from the grill and generously coat each piece with extra barbecue sauce. *Serves 4*

Summer Vegetable Stew over Blue Cornbread

*This fresh vegetable soup is a light, filling and actually very healthy way to start the day.
Enjoyed with the cornbread, it will keep you going until dinner. For those of you who don't eat
soup for breakfast, it serves as an extremely healthy and gratifying lunch or dinner.*

Mushroom Stock:
3 tablespoons extra virgin olive oil
1/2 pound shiitake mushrooms, coarsely chopped
1 pound domestic mushrooms, coarsely chopped
1 leek, coarsely chopped
1 carrot, coarsely chopped
3 garlic cloves, crushed
3 sprigs fresh basil
3 sprigs fresh parsley
Salt and freshly ground black pepper, to taste

Vegetable Stew:
4 to 6 shallots
1 carrot
1 small fennel bulb
2 to 3 potatoes
*1/4 small head cabbage (or bok choy,
    spinach, chard or other flavorful green)*
1/2 small eggplant
3 tablespoons olive oil
3 to 4 cloves garlic
6 to 10 fresh okra pods (optional)
2 large ripe tomatoes, peeled and seeded

*1/2 cup Cabernet Sauvignon or Zinfandel
    (optional)*
*1 1/2 tablespoons chopped fresh dill or
    1/4 cup chopped fresh basil*
Mushroom or chicken stock, to cover vegetables
Salt and freshly ground black pepper, to taste
1/4 pound snap beans, cut into 1/4-inch pieces
1 ear sweet corn, kernels removed

Blue Cornbread:
1 cup unbleached white flour
1 cup blue cornmeal
1/3 cup light brown sugar
1 1/2 tablespoons baking powder
1/2 teaspoon salt
2 eggs, slightly beaten
2 tablespoons grated red onion
1 tablespoon fresh jalapeño (optional)
2/3 cup grated cheddar cheese
2/3 cup fresh corn kernels
1 cup buttermilk
5 tablespoons unsalted butter, melted

In a 4- or 5-quart saucepan, heat oil and add all mushroom stock ingredients. Sauté for 10 minutes. Cover with 2 to 3 quarts of water and simmer over low heat until liquid is reduced by half. Add 2 cups of water and reduce again by half. Strain off the broth and season with salt and pepper. Discard the cooked vegetables.

The stock can be frozen in zip-lock bags for months. *Makes approximately 2 quarts of stock*

To make the stew, slice or chop shallots, carrot, fennel, potatoes, greens and eggplant into 1/2-inch pieces. In a 3- or 4-quart saucepan, sauté the vegetables in olive oil over medium heat for 10 minutes. Add the garlic

and okra, if desired, and continue to sauté for another 5 minutes. Add the tomatoes, wine, herbs and enough stock to cover the vegetables by at least 2 inches. Lower the heat and simmer for approximately 1 hour, or until the vegetables are tender. Add more stock along the way if the liquid reduces too much. Some people like a lot of broth and others make theirs more stew-like, so it's up to you. Do not add salt until the vegetables are completely cooked, because they will absorb it and you will end up using more salt than is needed.

Preheat the oven to 375 degrees F.

While the stew is cooking prepare the cornbread. In a medium bowl, combine the dry ingredients. In a large bowl, whisk the eggs together with the onion, chilies, cheese, corn, buttermilk and melted butter. Gradually blend the dry ingredients into the moist mixture. Do not overmix.

Pour the mixture into an oiled muffin pan. Bake for approximately 20 minutes or until muffins are firm at the center. Let cool for 10 minutes before removing from pans. *Makes 12 muffins*

While the cornbread is cooling, bring the soup back to a simmer. Add the beans and corn kernels and cook for approximately 2 to 3 minutes.

To serve, place a blue corn muffin in the center of a shallow soup bowl and ladle the soup around it. Sprinkle with a handful of lightly steamed fresh corn kernels. *Serves 4 to 6 generously*

Stewed Tomatoes with Potato Peasant Purses

*The flavors of the potatoes, cabbage and stewed tomatoes are as rustic as the presentation of
this dish. The purses can be made in advance, then warmed just before serving. Assemble the purses
and keep the stewed tomatoes warm in a pot. When ready to serve, place a heated purse on top
of a generous portion of tomatoes. A sprinkling of grated cheddar cheese on top is a perfect complement
to this dish. These purses go nicely served with grilled English-style sausages.*

Stewed Tomatoes:
1 medium yellow onion
1 small red or yellow bell pepper
1 stalk celery
2 tablespoons canola oil
3 pounds ripe tomatoes, coarsely chopped
5 to 7 sprigs fresh parsley
1/4 to 1/2 cup light brown sugar
Juice of 1 to 2 lemons
1 teaspoon salt
1/2 teaspoon freshly ground black pepper

Peasant Purses:
6 large cabbage leaves, preferably savoy
1 medium yellow onion, finely chopped
2 1/2 tablespoons unsalted butter (1/3 cup)
1/2 cup English peas (use frozen in a pinch)
2 tablespoons water
3 cups mashed potatoes
2 eggs, lightly beaten
Salt and freshly ground black pepper, to taste
12 green chives

Chop the onion, bell pepper and celery into 1/2-inch pieces. In a large stainless steel pot, sauté the vegetables in the oil over medium heat until translucent. Peel, seed and slice the tomatoes. Add tomatoes and parsley to the vegetables and cook covered over low heat for 20 minutes. Remove parsley sprigs. Season with 1/4 cup brown sugar, lemon juice, salt and pepper. Cook for 10 minutes longer and taste for seasoning. Add more sugar or salt, to taste. Keep warm until ready to serve.

In a 2-quart pot of boiling water, blanch the cabbage leaves until wilted; drain and cool. In a sauté pan over medium heat, sweat the onion in butter. Add peas and water, cover for 2 to 3 minutes. Remove cover. Cool slightly.

Meanwhile, in a large bowl, blend the mashed potatoes with eggs. Stir in the onion and pea mixture. Salt and pepper generously.

Flatten a cabbage leaf, cutting out any thick, unpliable stem. Place a generous 1/2 cup of potato mixture in the center of the leaf. Pull the leaves together, forming a pouch and tie with 2 chives. Just before serving, reheat the pouches for approximately 15 minutes in a steamer or a shallow pan of simmering water. Place each pouch on a plate covered with the warm stewed tomatoes. *Serves 3*

Penne with Sun-Dried Tomatoes, Asparagus and Smoked Trout in Goat Cheese Sauce

It's hard to fail with the flavor combinations in this pasta.
If you like your pasta a little saucier, add a few tablespoons of hot water.

12 whole shoots of spring garlic or baby leeks
2 teaspoons finely chopped garlic
1/3 cup extra virgin olive oil
1/4 to 1/2 cup sweet white wine
1/2 cup sun-dried tomatoes,
    soaked and coarsely chopped
6 to 8 ounces soft goat cheese

1 tablespoon finely chopped fresh thyme
1/4 cup toasted pine nuts
Salt and freshly ground black pepper, to taste
1 pound fresh asparagus,
    trimmed and cut into 2-inch pieces
8 to 10 ounces smoked trout (or salmon)
16 ounces fresh penne

In a large pot, bring approximately 3 quarts of salted water to a boil.

Meanwhile, cut off greens and tough parts of green garlic or leeks. Slice tender white part into 1/2-inch pieces. In a large sauté pan, slowly sauté both garlics with olive oil over medium heat until soft. Add the white wine and cook for 3 to 4 minutes. Add the tomatoes and crumble the goat cheese into the pan with the thyme and pine nuts. Season with salt and pepper. Cover and set aside.

Steam or boil asparagus in boiling water for approximately 3 minutes or until tender. Reserve boiling water to cook the pasta.

Bring the sauce back to heat. Break up the trout and add to the sauce. Turn off the heat.

Cook the penne in the boiling water for 2 to 3 minutes or until al dente. Drain and toss with the sauce. Place on a large platter or on individual plates and top or surround with the warm asparagus. *Serves 4*

Cappellini with Puttanesca Sauce

*I never seem to tire of this classic Italian tomato sauce. It is perfect
for pasta, combining both sweet and very salty flavors. I like to brown, then
stew chicken legs in the sauce and serve it over risotto or polenta.*

2 pounds ripe tomatoes
4 cloves garlic, finely chopped
1/2 to 1 teaspoon seeded and chopped chilies,
    such as serranos or jalapeños
1/4 cup extra virgin olive oil
2/3 cup Kalamata or good brine-cured olives, rinsed,
    pitted and chopped

4 to 5 whole anchovies, chopped
2 teaspoons finely chopped fresh oregano
2 tablespoons coarsely chopped fresh basil
2 or 3 tablespoons capers, drained

16 ounces cappellini (or other type of thin pasta,
    such as angel hair or vermicelli)

Peel, seed and chop the tomatoes, reserving any liquid for later use in thinning the sauce. In a large, heavy skillet, sauté the garlic, tomatoes and chilies in the olive oil over medium heat. Add remaining ingredients, lower heat and simmer for 10 minutes. If the sauce is too thick, thin with the reserved tomato juice or water. Cook the pasta in boiling, salted water until cooked al dente. Drain pasta and toss with a few teaspoons of olive oil. Put pasta on plates and top with a generous amount of the sauce.
Serves 4

Fresh Noodles with Just-Warmed Tomato Sauce

This tomato sauce recipe is so easy it is embarrassing. It is a reminder of how good food can be without much effort. In fact, it takes more time to make the noodles. For that matter, if you're pinched for time, purchase a package of fresh fettuccine from the store, but don't skimp on the sauce. It goes without saying that the tomatoes must be extraordinary for the finished dish to be the same.

Pasta Dough:
4 cups unbleached white flour
1 teaspoon salt
4 large eggs
Water, for dough to come together

Tomato Sauce:
1 small yellow onion, thinly sliced
3 cloves garlic, finely chopped

1/3 cup virgin olive oil
1/4 to 1/2 cup red wine
1 tablespoon coarsely chopped fresh oregano
1/4 cup coarsely chopped fresh parsley or basil
2 pounds ripe tomatoes, peeled, seeded and chopped
  (reserve any juices to add back into the sauce)
Salt and freshly ground black pepper, to taste

In a large bowl or on a large, flat surface, combine the flour and salt. Whisk eggs together and make a well in the center of the dry ingredients. Using your hands, gently blend the flour and eggs together. Add just enough water to form a stiff dough. Knead on a lightly floured board for approximately 10 minutes to form a smooth, elastic dough. Cover and let stand for approximately 30 minutes. Roll the dough very thin (using the 4 to 6 setting, depending on your pasta machine) and handcut into 1-inch strips. Toss noodles in plenty of flour to prevent them from sticking together.

In a heavy sauté pan, sauté the onion and garlic in olive oil over medium heat for approximately 5 minutes. Deglaze the pan with the red wine and add herbs. Warm another 3 to 4 minutes. Turn off heat and add the tomatoes to the sauté pan. Toss and season with salt and pepper. Add tomato juice or a bit of water to create a thinner sauce if you choose.

Cook noodles in a pot of boiling water. Because they are so fresh, it shouldn't take more than 2 to 3 minutes. Toss noodles with tomato sauce. Put sauced noodles on a large platter. For a Mexican touch, try garnishing the noodles with avocado slices, queso cheese and chopped cilantro. *Serves 4*

Fresh Tomato Lasagna over Wilted Greens

This lasagna is easy to put together because, rather than spending a lot of time
preparing a complex tomato sauce, you use sliced, fresh tomatoes.

White Sauce:
6 tablespoons unsalted butter
5 tablespoons unbleached white flour
2 cups milk
1/8 teaspoon freshly ground nutmeg
1/4 teaspoon salt

Lasagna:
1 1/2 pounds fresh ricotta
1/2 cup grated Italian grana cheese such as Asiago
1 teaspoon finely chopped fresh oregano
1 egg
1/2 to 1 teaspoon salt

Dash white pepper
1/4 cup pine nuts, toasted
8 ounces mozzarella cheese, cut into 1/4-inch cubes
8 ounces Provolone cheese, cut into 1/4-inch cubes
1 pound dry lasagna noodles or 1 1/2 pounds fresh
*   pasta sheets*
4 to 6 medium tomatoes, peeled, seeded and sliced
1/4 to 1/3 cup finely chopped fresh basil

2 tablespoons olive oil
1 teaspoon garlic, finely chopped
2 bunches chard, coarsely chopped

To prepare the white sauce, melt butter over medium heat in a saucepan. Whisk in the flour and cook, stirring constantly for 3 to 4 minutes. Continue to whisk, gradually adding the milk to the flour and butter, scraping the sides and bottom of the pan to avoid any lumps. Add nutmeg and salt. The sauce should have a consistency of thick pudding. Thin if necessary with a few extra tablespoons of milk.

In a large bowl, combine the ricotta, grated cheese, oregano, egg, salt, pepper and pine nuts. Add the mozzarella and Provolone.

Preheat the oven to 375 degrees F.

Meanwhile, cook pasta noodles in a large pot of boiling water for approximately 10 minutes or until al dente. Run the noodles under cold water. Drain and toss with a little olive oil to keep them from sticking.

Lightly coat a 3-quart baking dish with olive oil. Begin to layer the lasagna by placing a single layer of tomatoes with a generous sprinkling of basil on the bottom of the dish. Cover the tomatoes with layer of cooked pasta. Dollop half the ricotta mixture on top of the pasta sheets, top with another layer of cooked pasta, pressing down on the cheese to spread it evenly. Cover with 1 cup of the white sauce. Repeat the layering again, starting with the tomatoes. Cover the last layer with a generous sprinkle of grated cheese and bake for approximately 45 minutes or until the center of the lasagna is hot and bubbly.

Remove from oven and let stand for 15 to 20 minutes, to allow the lasagna to set.

Heat the olive oil and garlic. Add the chard, cover and turn off the heat.

Serve individual pieces of lasagna on top of the wilted chard. *Serves 4*

Herbed Pizza with Tomatoes, Ricotta, Shiitake Mushrooms and Onions

Tomatoes on pizza are a natural, but rather than using conventional cooked tomato sauce, use slices of fresh, juicy tomatoes. The moistness of the tomatoes and ricotta together create the most sensual pizza I've ever tasted.

Herbed Pizza Dough:
1 package dry yeast
3/4 cup warm water
1 teaspoon granulated sugar
1 tablespoon extra virgin olive oil
3 to 4 tablespoons finely chopped fresh herbs (such as basil, oregano, sage or rosemary)
1/2 teaspoon salt
2 1/4 cups unbleached white flour
1/4 cup whole wheat flour
Cornmeal for the pizza pan

1 medium yellow onion, thinly sliced
2 to 3 cloves garlic, finely chopped
1/4 pound shiitake mushrooms, thinly sliced, tough stems discarded
3 tablespoons extra virgin olive oil
3 tablespoons finely chopped fresh basil
1/2 teaspoon salt
1/4 teaspoon freshly ground black pepper
8 ounces fresh ricotta cheese
1 to 2 ripe tomatoes, sliced 1/4 inch thick
1/2 to 3/4 pound Provolone cheese, grated
1/4 cup grated Italian grana cheese (such as Asiago, aged Provolone or Pecorino)

In a small bowl, dissolve the yeast in the warm water until it turns frothy. Add the sugar, olive oil and herbs. On a wooden surface or in a food processor, blend the salt and the flours. Gradually work the flour and liquid together and knead for at least 5 minutes. Place in a well-oiled bowl and cover with a clean dish towel. Let rise in a warm place until doubled in size, approximately 45 minutes.

When the dough has risen, turn onto a floured board and roll out with a rolling pin to approximately 1/2-inch thickness. Lightly coat the pizza pan with cornmeal. Transfer dough onto the pizza pan.

Preheat the oven to 500 degrees F.

In a medium sauté pan, sauté the onions, garlic and mushrooms in the olive oil over medium heat. Add the basil and season with salt and pepper. Drain off any excess juice. Spread the vegetables evenly onto the pizza dough and top with small dollops of ricotta. Cover with tomato slices and sprinkle with cheese. Bake for approximately 15 minutes or until pizza crust is light brown and cheese is bubbly. *Serves 2 to 4*

BAKED GOODS

We don't often think of tomatoes as ingredients for baking. This chapter is meant to inspire and take you beyond your limits. Tomatoes have their acknowledged place on pizza, but how about in a pie or an old-fashioned baked betty?

Some cooks still consider tomatoes a fruit rather than a vegetable. After baking the Tomato Ginger Upside-Down Cake, you will understand why. Try to think of unripe green tomatoes as you would crisp, tart cooking apples. Incorporate them into some of your favorite apple recipes. Keep in mind that you may need to increase the amount of sugar or spices to accommodate the lack of sweetness in the tomato.

Take into consideration the water content of ripe, juicy tomatoes, and play it safe by draining off excess liquids before incorporating tomatoes into a recipe. Or, dust the tomatoes with a seasoned flour before adding to a cake or quick bread.

Sun-dried tomatoes can be as sweet as raisins. If the original, fresh tomato is full of sugar and flavor, its dried counterpart will be the same, but with even more intensity. Sun-Dried Tomato Biscuits are a fabulous addition to a Sunday brunch or afternoon tea.

When browsing through baking books, keep the prospect of sweet or green tomatoes as an ingredient tucked away in the back of your mind. You may be surprised at what transpires.

Tomato Brie Bread Pudding

Even mentioning tomatoes in bread pudding brings looks of chagrin. I know if I could get the skeptics to take just one bite they would be sold forever.

6 lightly packed cups of soft white bread
1 yellow onion, coarsely chopped
2 stalks celery, coarsely chopped
1 1/2 sticks unsalted butter
1 teaspoon salt, or to taste
1/4 teaspoon white pepper
2 pounds ripe tomatoes, seeded and coarsely chopped
8 ounces Brie cheese, cut into 1/2-inch pieces
3 eggs, lightly beaten
2 to 3 cups chicken or vegetable stock,
   homemade or canned

Preheat the oven to 350 degrees F.

Break bread into small pieces and place in a large bowl. In a medium saucepan, sauté the onions and celery in the butter over medium heat. Season with salt and pepper. Pour the sautéed mixture over the bread and toss.

Butter a 2-quart baking dish. Spread a layer of the bread mixture on the bottom. Cover with a layer of tomatoes and a third of the cheese. Continue layering, ending up with a layer of the bread mixture on top.

In a small bowl, whisk together the eggs and 1 cup of the chicken stock. Pour over the dish. All the bread should be lightly moistened. Add more stock if necessary. Sprinkle remaining cheese on top. Bake for approximately 35 minutes or until pudding is fluffy, firm and golden brown. Let stand for 10 minutes before serving. This bread pudding is also great when served at room temperature. *Serves 6*

Green Tomato Brown Betty

This is a glorious way to use those green tomatoes left on the vine that will never ripen. The layering process in this recipe is what makes it a betty.

2 cups crumbs (graham crackers,
   whole wheat cracker or cookie crumbs)
1 stick unsalted butter, melted
3 pounds (approximately 3 1/2 cups)
   unripe green tomatoes, thinly sliced
3/4 cup raisins
Juice of 1 lemon
1 1/4 cups light brown sugar
1 tablespoon cinnamon
1 teaspoon ground allspice
1/2 cup apple juice

Preheat the oven to 350 degrees F.

In a small bowl, combine the crumbs and melted butter. Set aside. In a medium bowl, mix the tomatoes, raisins, lemon juice, sugar and spices together.

Butter a 2-quart baking dish. Spread a third of the crumb mixture evenly over the bottom. Spread half of the tomato mixture on top of the crumbs. Sprinkle with half the apple juice. Cover with another third of the crumb mixture, followed by the remaining tomatoes. Sprinkle with the rest of the apple juice. Finish by covering the tomatoes with the remaining crumb mixture.

Cover and bake for approximately 45 minutes or until the tomatoes are soft. Remove the cover. Raise the heat to 400 degrees F. and bake for another 10 minutes or until browned on top. Serve hot with ice cream. *Serves 6*

Green Tomato Brown Betty

Sun-Dried Tomato Biscuits

*Sweet, delicate and moist, these buttermilk biscuits
are a perfect accompaniment to a bowl of stew.*

2 cups unbleached white flour
1 tablespoon baking powder
1 tablespoon granulated sugar
1 teaspoon salt
1 stick unsalted butter, frozen
2 eggs
1/2 cup buttermilk
1/3 cup sun-dried tomatoes, finely chopped
1 tablespoon finely chopped fresh thyme

Preheat the oven to 400 degrees F.

In a large bowl, sift together the dry
ingredients. Finely chop the butter. By hand or
in a food processor, blend with the dry ingredients. The mixture should not be thoroughly
blended, but should have small, pea-sized
clumps of butter and flour.

In a small bowl, whisk the eggs and buttermilk together. Stir in the sun-dried tomatoes
and thyme. Using the pulse of the food processor or just your hands, work together the dry
and moist ingredients until the dough begins
to come together. Do not overwork or your
biscuits will be tough.

Turn the dough onto a floured board and
roll to 1/2-inch thickness. Fold in half and roll
out again. Fold in half one more time and
roll to 3/4-inch thickness. Cut the dough into
2-inch-square biscuits. Bake in the oven on a
lightly oiled baking sheet for approximately 12
minutes or until biscuits are fluffy and browned.
Makes approximately 12 biscuits

Tomato Spice Tea Bread

*This recipe was given to me by Beth Hensperger,
author, teacher and bread-baking expert.
Once you gather the ingredients, the bread is
prepared and baked within an hour.*

2 large ripe, red tomatoes
2 eggs
1/3 cup vegetable oil
1/2 cup granulated sugar
1/2 cup light brown sugar
1 1/2 cups unbleached white flour
1 teaspoon ground cinnamon
1/2 teaspoon baking powder
Pinch of salt
1/4 cup sliced almonds

Peel and seed the tomatoes. Place in a blender
or food processor with a metal blade and
coarsely purée. Measure out 1 1/4 cups purée.

With an electric mixer, blend the eggs, oil
and sugars. Beat at high speed for approximately 3 minutes or until batter is light and
fluffy. Add the tomato purée and mix well.

In a large bowl, combine all the dry ingredients except the almonds and add gradually
to the moist. Beat at medium speed until
thoroughly blended. The batter will be thin.

Grease a 6-cup Bundt pan or an 8-inch
loaf pan. Pour the batter evenly into the pan.
Sprinkle the top with almonds. Bake for approximately 40 minutes or until a skewer
inserted into the center of the bread comes out
clean. Cool in pan for 5 minutes, turn out on
a rack and cool before cutting into thin slices.
Makes 1 loaf; Serves 6 to 8

Green Tomato Raspberry Pie

*You need to use plenty of sugar for this pie but the combination of
sweet raspberries and tangy green tomatoes is truly delicious. This recipe makes an oversized pie,
the kind I envision sitting on the windowsill of Gramma's house.*

My Favorite Pie Dough:
  (for a double-crusted, 10-inch glass pie plate)
2 sticks unsalted butter
2 1/2 cups unbleached all-purpose flour
1/2 teaspoon salt
8 rounded tablespoons sour cream

8 cups unripe green tomatoes,
   cut into thin wedges or slices

2 small baskets red raspberries or blackberries
1 tablespoon lemon zest
3/4 cup granulated sugar
1 cup light brown sugar
1/4 cup cornstarch (or more, if berries are very juicy)
2 teaspoons ground cinnamon
1/2 teaspoon freshly grated nutmeg (optional)
6 tablespoons unsalted butter

To prepare the pie dough, cut the butter into 10 chunks with a knife. In a small bowl, combine the flour and salt. By hand or in a food processor, coarsely blend the butter, flour and salt. Add the sour cream to the butter-flour mixture in small dollops. Blend until dough begins to come together.

Turn onto a lightly floured board. Divide in half and form into 2 even balls. Set 1 ball aside. Flatten the other ball, dusting both sides lightly with flour to prevent sticking. Roll the dough to approximately 1/8-inch thickness. The outer perimeter should be approximately 2 inches beyond the edge of a 10-inch pie plate. Press dough into pie plate, leaving the edges uncut until you roll out the top crust.

Roll out the other ball of dough. Place between 2 pieces of waxed paper or a flour-dusted dish towel. Fold in half and store it with the lower crust in the refrigerator until the filling is prepared.

Preheat oven to 400 degrees F.

In a large bowl, combine the tomatoes, blackberries and lemon zest. In a small bowl, combine the sugars, cornstarch and spices. Toss all the ingredients together and heap the mixture into the lined pie plate. Dot with chunks of butter. Cover with the top pastry crust, crimp edges together and bake in the oven for 10 minutes.

Reduce heat to 350 degrees F. Bake for approximately 40 minutes longer or until the crust is lightly browned and when you test the middle of the pie with a toothpick, the tomatoes feel very soft.

Remove from the oven and cool for at least 30 minutes before cutting. Serve warm with vanilla ice cream. Makes a big, beautiful, 10-inch pie. *Serves 8*

Tomato Ginger Upside-Down Cake

*I adapted this recipe from an eighteenth century cookbook,
one of many that my dear friend Lisa Fenwick has sent my way.*

1 stick unsalted butter, melted
1 tablespoon grated fresh ginger
6 tablespoons light brown sugar
2 to 3 ripe tomatoes (or enough to cover the
 bottom of the pan as you would a pineapple
 upside-down cake), skinned, seeded and
 sliced 1/4 inch thick
1 stick unsalted butter

1 1/2 cups brown sugar
1/2 cup molasses
2 1/2 cups unbleached white flour
2 teaspoons baking powder
1 tablespoon ground ginger
1/2 teaspoon ground cloves
1 cup buttermilk

Preheat the oven to 350 degrees F.

Combine the melted butter with the ginger and sugar and spread evenly on the bottom of a 10-inch by 14-inch baking pan. Cover with tomato slices.

Meanwhile, in a mixer, cream the butter with the brown sugar and molasses. In another bowl, sift together the flour, baking powder and spices. Add flour mixture alternately with the buttermilk to the creamed butter and sugar. Pour batter over tomatoes in baking pan.

Bake for approximately 40 minutes or until a toothpick comes out clean when testing the center of the cake. Remove from the oven, loosen outer edges with a knife and invert onto a platter larger than the baking pan. Let stand at least 5 minutes before trying to remove the pan. Serve warm with whipped cream or vanilla ice cream. *Serves 6 or more*

METRIC CONVERSIONS

Liquid Weights

U.S. Measurements	Metric Equivalents
1/4 teaspoon	1.23 ml
1/2 teaspoon	2.5 ml
3/4 teaspoon	3.7 ml
1 teaspoon	5 ml
1 dessertspoon	10 ml
1 tablespoon (3 teaspoons)	15 ml
2 tablespoons (1 ounce)	30 ml
1/4 cup	60 ml
1/3 cup	80 ml
1/2 cup	120 ml
2/3 cup	160 ml
3/4 cup	180 ml
1 cup (8 ounces)	240 ml
2 cups (1 pint)	480 ml
3 cups	720 ml
4 cups (1 quart)	1 litre
4 quarts (1 gallon)	3 3/4 litres

Dry Weights

U.S. Measurements	Metric Equivalents
1/4 ounce	7 grams
1/3 ounce	10 grams
1/2 ounce	14 grams
1 ounce	28 grams
1 1/2 ounces	42 grams
1 3/4 ounces	50 grams
2 ounces	57 grams
3 ounces	85 grams
3 1/2 ounces	100 grams
4 ounces (1/4 pound)	114 grams
6 ounces	170 grams
8 ounces (1/2 pound)	227 grams
9 ounces	250 grams
16 ounces (1 pound)	464 grams

Temperatures

Farenheit	Celsius (Centigrade)
32°F (water freezes)	0°C
200°F	95°C
212°F (water boils)	100°C
250°F	120°C
275°F	135°C
300°F (slow oven)	150°C
325°F	160°C
350°F (moderate oven)	175°C
375°F	190°C
400°F (hot oven)	205°C
425°F	220°C
450°F (very hot oven)	230°C
475°F	245°C
500°F (extremely hot oven)	260°C

Length

U.S. Measurements	Metric Equivalents
1/8 inch	3 mm
1/4 inch	6 mm
3/8 inch	1 cm
1/2 inch	1.2 cm
3/4 inch	2 cm
1 inch	2.5 cm
1 1/4 inches	3.1 cm
1 1/2 inches	3.7 cm
2 inches	5 cm
3 inches	7.5 cm
4 inches	10 cm
5 inches	12.5 cm

Approximate Equivalents

1 kilo is slightly more than 2 pounds
1 litre is slightly more than 1 quart
1 meter is slightly over 3 feet
1 centimeter is approximately 3/8 inch

INDEX